SENSIBLY THIN®

Low-Fat Living and Cooking

Volume I

Dedication

For my dear friend **Mary Ann**, whom I admire
and deeply love. Without you I would not have
had my first client. Many thanks, Mary Ann, for
believing in me and for those special words,
"You can do it Sam."

Acknowledgments

A huge thanks to the following people for all of their assistance in making this dream come true. It could not have been done without any of you!

To my staff and friends:
Jean Bassett
Suzanne Bracewell
Pat Hanson
Kim Kildal
Ann Shook
Teresa Sonsthagen
Sharon Trieglaff Jons
Leslie VanLaningham - Boy, am I glad you did not know what you were getting into.
Maureen Weeks - Who listened and helped me, even in St. Maarten.
Ann Williams
LeAnn Zogg
Clients of Sensibly Thin -- for the recipes!

Table of Contents

Introduction

Welcome to **SENSIBLY THIN** and congratulations on your decision toward healthy weight management. People who join **SENSIBLY THIN** are here for reasons other than to just look slimmer. Some are referred by their physician to control their cholesterol, diabetes, or assist with eating disorders.

> *Sam's Note:*
> *Some people who look thin may have experienced a worse pain than those of us that have experienced the pain of being overweight.*

When prospective clients call us about our weight loss program we are often asked, "How long will it take me to lose weight?" We have all heard a thousand times, that to lose more than two pounds per week is unsafe. (Boring, Boring, Boring) Do we really understand why this is true? **There are 3500 calories in one pound of body fat. To lose two pounds you must burn (3,500 x 2) or 7,000 more calories than you consume. Two pounds. Yahoo!! What an accomplishment** The body can only burn fat safely at this speed! Unless you are into a strict combination of diet and exercise, drastic cuts in calories will cause you to burn muscle instead of fat. (Oh No! Not That!) A quick weight loss takes valuable tissue from your body. It burns muscle, not only from visible areas, but also from the body's most vital organs!

Not every person will fit a certain weight determined by a chart. (Darn!) That is why charts are not found in this book. Of the three weights given in a weight chart, people will usually choose the lowest weight. At one time I got to my lowest goal on a weight chart, but I looked too thin and I could not keep the weight off. (Look Ma! No hips! No boobs either!)

As a result, I became frustrated and regained all my weight plus 30 pounds more within one year! It took me years to give up all the magic and gimmicks and realize that I had to change certain behaviors and eating habits forever.

I have accepted the fact that I can no longer have a jar of chocolate chip cookies in my home. What would you choose after a long day, an apple or a cookie? Because sugar tastes so good, it can be easy to overload on. Desserts have empty calories that are fun to eat as a treat, but remember that anything eaten in excess isn't good for us! (Boo!) That does not mean that I can never have a cookie. When I do choose to bring them home, I bring one for each family member and enjoy every bite without guilt! Use sweets for what they are -- a dessert.

My weight loss theory is simple, **overeat equals overweight.** It's simple **but not always easy** to control. These three things are the keys to a permanent weight loss and a healthy life style.

1. A well-balanced diet that meets the needs of your body and your lifestyle.

2. Behavior modification to change your thinking and eating habits so you will remain thin after your weight loss.

Sam's Note: *It takes from 6 months to 2 years to change our behavior. Well Holy Cow! I am the first to wish it were faster.*

3. An exercise program that promotes weight loss and a good cardiovascular workout. (Whew!) We encourage 30 minutes of exercise three times a week. **Be flexible with exercise.** What works for one will not necessarily work for someone else.

Once again, Welcome to **SENSIBLY THIN.**

Editor's Note

Welcome to the **Sensibly Thin** cookbook! As editor of the cookbook, and a client at **Sensibly Thin,** I have learned may things. A few of these I need to share with you. As you read the cookbook understand that we assume a few simple things. Use light and low-calorie products when called for. Always, always, always, use skinless chicken, and boneless, skinless chicken breasts! While reading through the exchanges if you see **HFB** it means this exchange is a high fat bread. In other words, it could have been a bread and a fat, but because it is "walking the thin line" between the two, we choose to simplify matters and call it a high fat bread.

At **Sensibly Thin** we believe that weight control does not consist of simply eating, cooking and exercising correctly. In today's world we are all faced with an abundance of challenges. The following lecture is a beginning of the many reasons why people overeat.

COMPULSIVE OVEREATING
The Food Trap
Sam Eukel, Owner of Sensibly Thin

Although Anorexia and Bulimia have long since been recognized as eating disorders, it is only recently that Compulsive Overeating has been recognized as an eating disorder, and it's about time!

Compulsive Overeating may be the result of habits, obsessions, food addictions, or any combination of these. An individual may display one or more of these causative factors, or perhaps none of them. If a person is overweight and constantly losing and regaining 10 to 100 pounds, food is being used to fulfill a need. A compulsion has been created. Having a compulsion with food is a serious problem.

A habit is a learned behavior. We are all familiar with Pavlov's experiments where he trained dogs to salivate by ringing a bell every time food was presented. After a short time the bell was rung and the dog salivated without the food stimulus. Think about how we are conditioned to eat in front of the television. The television becomes our "bell" and we begin to salivate. A certain program comes on, such as Sunday football, and off we go to get our food and settle in for the afternoon. These are learned behaviors or habits that can be changed.

It only takes three times to form a habit, but **eleven consecutive** times to change one. It takes six months to two years to implement a behavior change. The 10-15 pounds that a person continually loses and regains are usually the result of poor habits.

To learn new behaviors, or to learn why we are overeating can be difficult, but not impossible. Many overweight people have sought help with weight loss only to receive a piece of paper that instructs them to eat 1200 calories per day. A piece of paper and a one-time visit does not provide the support or the knowledge to lose weight and keep it off. The difficulty is trying to do it alone. Most people need help changing behaviors and losing the unwanted weight for good.

Maybe we have a goal weight and a goal date in mind and clench our fists to begin. We promise ourselves that when we get thin, we'll never gain the weight again. We believe all will be "fixed", life will be perfect. In reality the fat is not the problem, the fat is a symptom of the problem.

Maybe we think we can mobilize our will power and fight for as long as is needed. However, the belief that, "All I need is a little more willpower" only brings guilt and self-loathing. Sometimes the pressure of dieting or cutting down on eating actually increases the tension and desire for food. Many overweight people have learned that sharing their feelings is not safe, so an emotional outlet is developed through food. Eating serves to mask or repress feelings. When we attempt to remove or limit food, which has served as our coping mechanism, intense feelings start to bubble to the surface. This may explain why people who diet are moody?

Many people, as they gain weight, try a new hair style or an eye catching outfit hoping no one will notice their body. For most people, moving from a size 12 to a size 24, or having a closet full of clothing in many sizes makes them recognize that they have gained weight. **This is not** necessarily true for the Compulsive Overeater. Most Compulsive Overeaters do not have a realistic sense of their own body and consistently underestimate their size. They are aware of the pounds on the scale, and don't like it, therefore they choose not to see the pounds in the mirror. That is why, when we see a picture of ourselves in a video we often cry, "Is that me? Am I really that heavy?"

There are many definitions for the term "Compulsive Overeating." Some describe it as an addiction. Unfortunately, the word "addiction" often connotates weakness, lack of willpower, and the inability to face problems. The positive part of labeling oneself as having an "addiction" is that it enables one to let go of control issues, to trust someone other than oneself, and to identify a starting point for one's recovery.

The word "addicted" means to surrender oneself to a practice or habit, even if it is hurtful. The answer is not in trying to "control" the addiction or "white knuckling it," but in being aware of one's powerlessness. Surrender is facing the truth that one may not be in control of food, that is why it is an addiction. It takes more than willpower to combat an addiction. Education, time and counseling are all necessary. It is paramount that we understand what all addictions and compulsions have in common: the out- of-control and aimless search for wholeness, happiness and peace.

Although there are many kinds of addictions and compulsions, the theme is the same. A person engages in a relationship with an object, an activity, or a substance in order to produce a desired mood change. That object might be gambling, shopping, tobacco, alcohol, food or sex.

For the Compulsive Overeater, consuming food causes an emotional shift. Overeating creates temporary feelings of relaxation, excitement, or being in control. Overeating is also a way of escaping from feelings produced by the pressures and stresses of everyday life. The overeater may even come to believe that food is an escape from the shame and guilt created by being overweight. They may then eat more saying, "I've already blown it so I might as well continue eating." The overeating leads to more overeating and more shame, etc.

Compulsive Overeating locks the overeater into a cycle of emotionally avoiding life. For example, a Compulsive Overeater may binge after a fight with a friend or a partner and find the illusion of peace. For the moment they feel full instead of empty, but only for a **short** while. During these moments there is a sense of comfort, solace and peace of mind. Individuals enter into this emotional relationship with food in order to meet unfulfilled needs. The interaction between the person and the food may occur many times before they realize a relationship has been formed. Emotional needs often feel urgent and emotional logic works to satisfy this urgency, even if it is not in the person's best interest. Emotional logic cries, "I want what I want, and I want it now!"

It would not be socially acceptable for a recovering alcoholic to serve wine with a meal. Yet the Compulsive Overeater continues to serve, or be served, their favorite dessert without any social stigma. Food is served at all kinds of social gatherings; weddings, coffee parties, card clubs, funerals and celebrations of all kinds. The basic function of food is to nourish the body. The overeater departs from the basic function of food and develops a relationship with food, attempting to meet personal needs.

Most individuals eat to appease hunger. However, the Compulsive Overeater gets misled. Something triggers overeating and food is used for more than nourishment. The trigger might be trauma, anxiety, or boredom. Food becomes a psychological crutch with which the overeater attempts to deal with pain, frustration and feelings. The mood change accompanying overeating is predictable and consistent. Food has no wants or needs and makes no demands on the eater. Food does not yell back, criticize, or walk away. In a relationship with food, the overeater can always come first. This is not true in a relationship with friends or family, where others needs and wants are concerned.

The Compulsive Overeater and food addict often avoids responsibility by staying in a denial stage. The following rationalizations may throw a Compulsive Overeater off track and cause them to become susceptible to addiction.

- I'm still hovering within my weight range.
- This food in my mouth has nothing to do with the fat on my body.
- My scale is broken.
- The dryer is shrinking my clothes.
- I can go on a diet and lose weight whenever I want.
- This is no big deal; I can handle it myself. All I need is willpower.
- I'm so accomplished in other areas of my life, I don't need to worry about this. Life is too short.
- It's not my fault. Who wouldn't eat with husband/wife/mother/father/children like mine?
- I have to eat this way to maintain my job.
- How can I eat so little and not lose weight?
- I guess it's only water retention.
- If I were a stronger person, I would lose weight.

By gorging themselves, the overeater creates the temporary illusion of control. Food addiction is buying into false and empty promises. The promise of relief, emotional security and the false sense of fulfillment is merely an illusion.

Emotionally, the Compulsive Overeater may confuse intimacy with intensity. Food addicts may run to the store to buy special foods to alter their mood, eat, then feel guilty and loathsome. This is an "intense" experience, however, the individual may have been seeking intimacy. Once again the overeater uses food to fulfill needs. Addiction makes life lonely and creates more of a need to act out through eating. This results in shame which perpetuates the vicious cycle.

Adolescents live for the moment, as do Compulsive Overeaters, "emotional logic" justifies food abuse. Often an addicted individual will be described as adolescent in both behavior and attitude. The difference is that adolescents grow up, while addicts stay trapped in an adolescent stage. As long as the addict's disease is not in control, they remain stuck.

The incidence of Compulsive Overeating will continue to grow as long as we remain ignorant of the dangers of food addiction. Learning to eat properly is a major accomplishment. There is no magic pill or gimmick in weight loss. No matter what your size, it takes behavior modification, considerable time, and sustained motivation to change habits and attitudes for good. It takes a lifetime commitment, not just a temporary effort. It is sometimes easier to stay stuck than it is to explore the reasons we overeat. In order to make permanent changes we must understand and accept how and why we have become overweight. And we need to forgive ourselves.

For more information about joining **Sensibly Thin's** 800 Program, call 1-800-977-5779.

References

American Psychiatric Association; Diagnostic and Statistical Manual of Mental Disorders, Third Edition, Revised. Washington, D.C., American Psychiatric Association, 1987.

Glasser, W. (1984). Take Effective Control of Your Life. New York: Harper and Row.

Hollis, J. (1985). Fat is a Family Affair. San Francisco: Harper and Row.

Nakken, C. (1988). The Addictive Personality: Understanding Compulsions in Our Lives. San Francisco: Harper and Row.

Woody, R.H. (1980). Encyclopedia of Clinical Assessment. San Francisco: Jossey-Bass.

Dining Out Survival

Contrary to what many people believe, it is entirely possible to dine out and lose weight. I work with clients who travel all week and have learned to order all three meals in restaurants. Dining out need not be a license to overeat. In fact, it can be better in many ways than staying home and nibbling from the minute we begin to prepare a meal right through cleanup.

The following are five basic skills you will need to practice in order to make dining out a healthy, pleasurable experience:

1. **Plan ahead.** As often as possible be the one to choose the restaurant and know in advance what you will order. Avoid menu shopping. You probably know the menu better than the owner does. Don't even open it! If you plan in advance, you will be less tempted.
2. **Avoid under eating. Don't eat so little prior to going out that you end up eating anything that is not nailed down!** Most people do not order milk and fruit when they dine out. I suggest having a cup of sugar-free hot cocoa and a piece of fruit before leaving home. It will save many calories in the long run.
3. **Monitor the fats.** Remove the "F" word from your diet vocabulary. No **"fried" or "free"** foods!
4. **Make special requests.** Do not be embarrassed to ask many questions. Send food back if it is not prepared the way you request.

5. Use portion control. Ask for a doggie bag and enjoy the **leftovers for lunch the next day.** Restaurant portions are usually large enough to feed two, so why not split a meal?

Remember:
* 1 Tbsp. of salad dressing = 1 fat,
* The size of a deck of cards = 3 oz. portion of meat
* 1/2 cup of potatoes or pasta = 1 bread

Chinese

As an appetizer, you could choose one cup of egg drop soup, won ton soup or hot and sour soup. No more "F" word appetizers such as **fried** won tons, egg rolls or chicken wings. Do you really believe restaurants can make fresh appetizers and fry them as quickly as they do after you place your order? More likely they are already fried once then dunked in hot grease again for reheating!

Chinese food portions are very large, the main course can definitely be split. Stir fried is always best. Ask for broth instead of oil to be used to stir fry. If you have high blood pressure or bloat easily, hold the MSG.

Nuts are high in fat. Two whole walnuts or four cashews are fifty calories. How many cashews are usually in a stir fry order? Also, if the dish has nuts it contains less vegetables.

Stay away from sweet and sour dishes, they are battered and deep fried! If you enjoy sweet and sour, find a recipe and prepare it at home. Sweet and sour is in the sauce. Food does not need to be deep fried to accompany it!

Fried rice contains what letter? Order steamed rice only. Ever tried chopsticks? They slow down your eating! Enjoy the fortune cookie, it is only 25 calories.

Mexican

Follow these suggestions and Mexican meals will be much easier to order.

Corn chips have two "F" words, "fried" and "free"! Chips may not be a monetary burden but you'll pay dearly later. Ten chips are a high fat bread exchange, 125 calories. How many chips come in a basket - 50, 100? How many times does the basket get filled? You could eat 1,000 to 2,000 calories in chips alone! More than likely, you are not going to want to skip the chips entirely so what are your options?

1. How many chips do you eat while waiting for your meal? Ask the waiter not to bring them until the meal is served. This works best when dining with an understanding friend or spouse.
2. Count out ten chips, break them in half, which will give you twenty. Eat them with the hand you don't normally eat with to slow the process. Consider wearing a white shirt you don't want to spill on and watch how that little trick will slow your eating down!
3. Ask the waiter to bring only half a basket of chips and remove them when the meal comes.
4. A word about Salsa. It is only 25 calories per half cup, but is high in sodium. The real problem is what you eat the Salsa with!

Here are some wonderful Mexican food choices:

- A tostada with beans, beef or chicken, a little melted cheese, topped with lettuce and Salsa. Skip the soggy shell and have ten crisp chips.
  The exchanges are: 3 protein, 1 bread

- A taco salad without the shell is a good choice. The shell alone, depending on the size, is 250-500 calories. If you MUST have the shell, eat the upper 1 inch that isn't soggy and add one bread exchange.
  The exchanges are: 3-4 protein, 1vegetable.
- Most burritos are big enough for two people! Have the gravy served on the side (50 calories per Tbsp.). This allows you to control how much you use. The gravy will probably come in a cereal size bowl. Can you believe it? That really is how much gravy is poured over a burrito!
  The exchanges are: 3 protein, 1 bread (1/2 burrito).
- A fajita is great! Ask for the vegetables or meat to be stir fried without the oil. The only reason the oil is poured on top in the first place is so it will sizzle when they bring it out. Don't worry it will still be hot. Hold the sour cream and guacamole! If 1/8 of a avocado is a fat exchange at 50 calories, then imagine mixing it with mayonnaise, 1/4 cup is 200 calories.
  The exchanges are: 2 protein, 1 bread, 1 vegetable.
- Ironically, the best chicken I've ever ordered came from a Mexican restaurant. It is seasoned wonderfully and is usually served with a salad and Spanish rice.
  Exchanges are: 3 protein, 1 bread, 1 vegetable.

What about a jumbo Margarita at 500-700 calories each? Does three shots of tequila and syrup taste that good? That's a lot of calories that you can't even chew!

Italian

A basic rule to remember is **no white sauce!**
Fettucini Alfredo has 1500 calories a serving. Tomato
based meals are by far the more health and calorie
conscious choice. Most Italian restaurants today will serve
half portions or luncheon portions in the evening. At least,
make the choice to split the entree with a companion. If
you order a chicken dish, be sure to ask the waiter to have
the skin removed before cooking. Italians make wonderful
bread. Bread sticks weigh two ounces each and can easily
contain 300 calories. Why? They are brushed with garlic
oil before baking! Now what about the butter you add!
Here are some options you can try:

1. No bread at all.
2. Eat only half your bread stick when the bread is brought
   to the table, then eat the other half when the basket gets
   passed around again.
3. Move the basket away from you.
4. Cut the bread into fourths and have three pieces with
   your salad and one piece with your meal.
5. Ask your server to bring the bread without butter! You
   may have to wait a few extra minutes, but you will have
   the freshest bread! Do not forget there are doggie bags
   available in Italian restaurants!

Pizza

Two slices of pizza equal 3 protein and 2 bread
exchanges. Remember this is a gift! Order a salad with the
dressing on the side to help fill in for an extra slice of
pizza. If you were wondering whether deep dish pizza fits
into that exchange. Think again! Oh, you were teasing of
course!

Pizza is high in nutrition if you order correctly and don't overeat. Cheese, vegetable or Canadian Bacon with any combination of fruits or vegetables and maybe even some black olives are all good choices.

I do not know of another meal where you only eat the entree. When you serve a steak, chicken or pork you serve a side dish and other accompaniment? So, why don't we have a salad with our pizza? It will help to fill you up and slow you down. If you order a pizza at home, you could have a salad, cut up some fresh fruits, and have a glass of milk. If you are going out for pizza, grab a piece of fruit on the way to stave off your hunger before you get to the restaurant.

Does your family insist on pepperoni or Italian sausage? Pizza establishments offer half and half pizza. I guarantee that after your family finishes their high-fat, high calorie half, they will help you eat your pizza. No matter what you decided to order. If you are tempted to sample theirs, take two or three paper napkins and press out the grease from the pepperoni, sausage, or hamburger on the top of the pizza.

Seafood

Seafood ranges from healthy to decadently high in fat and cholesterol. Seafood is among the healthiest protein foods available. Even salmon, which is a high calorie fish, is only 40 calories per ounce. But, (there's always a but!) fish's nutrition pluses can be destroyed if it is prepared using high calorie ingredients.

Even shrimp, which used to be considered a high cholesterol food, is recommended and accepted today because it is so low in saturated fat. If you have high cholesterol, enjoy shrimp in controlled portions. Three to four ounces, once in a while, is approved by the American

Heart Association.

I am amazed at how few people realize the word "sauté" means fried. Deep fried means dumped in oil and cooked. Sautéed means fried in butter on the stove. You are at the mercy of the person who is sautéing. How much margarine or butter they use determines how many calories you eat.

Any fish is great, **BUT**, ask how it is prepared. If butter is used, ask them to broil your fish choice using lemon only, and to bring lemon wedges. Avoid fries. Ask for a baked potato with sour cream and margarine on the side. Order a salad with dressing on the side. **Do not** pour dressing on top! Dunk the tines of the fork into the dressing, then take a bite of the lettuce. Twice the taste; half the calories.

Skip the coleslaw! Why take such a low calorie food (cabbage) and mix it with fat and calories? (1/2 cup coleslaw = 1 vegetable and 2 fats)

If fish is fresh, it should not have an offensive ammonia odor. Fish contains mostly water. It make sense when you consider where they live! If fish is dry, it has lost too much water by being overcooked.

There are many healthy ways to order fish: broiled, steamed, grilled. marinated in teriyaki, or tomato sauce, stir fried with chicken broth, or wine, topped with herbs, Parmesan cheese, paprika, or blackened cajun style.
Note: I did not recommend batter dipped, fried, breaded, or served with white sauce! For the healthiest meal order:
1. 3 ounces of any fish = 3 protein
2. baked potato = 1 bread
3. salad is a free exchange
4. 2 Tbsp. sour cream = 1 fat
5. 1 Tbsp reduced calorie dressing = 1 fat
6. Non-alcoholic beverage

American

This is certainly a place where questions need to be asked. If you end up in a small restaurant where you do not think there is anything you can order, **do not** open the menu and begin menu shopping. Most restaurants serve a beef or turkey sandwich. Order the beef or turkey with a scoop of mashed potatoes, gravy on the side. You decide if you want to add margarine. Yes, often the only vegetables offered are peas or corn. Neither would be such a horrible choice if that was all that is available. After all, it would look pretty sad to have just meat and potatoes. Of course, you could always add a tossed salad to this meal. Not a bad meal for a restaurant where you were thinking there wouldn't be anything to order!

My *pet peeve*, croissant sandwiches. Some croissants contain as much as 5 tsp. of fat for 220 calories, plus 160 calories in bread, for a total of 380 calories per croissant! That is without the filling, which is usually mayo-based and adds at least 50 calories from the mayonnaise alone. Now you are up to 430 calories and that doesn't include the meat. Yikes! When are restaurants going to wise up and stop serving those croissant sandwiches and a cup of creamed soup?

Diet plates, what a joke! Who thought this one up?
4 oz Hamburger = 300 calories
1/2 cup Cottage cheese = 100 calories
Hard boiled egg = 100 calories
Slice of toast = 75 calories
Total calories = 575
Talk about "I could have had a V8"!

You could have had:
4 oz. Sirloin Steak = 220 calories
Baked potato = 80 calories
Salad = free
reduced calorie dressing, 1 Tbsp = 40 calories
Margarine, 1 pat = 45 calories
Total calories = 390

Special requests American style:
- Please bring the salad dressing and/or syrup on the side. (Dip the tines of the fork in the dressing or syrup, then take a bite. Twice the taste with half the calories)!
- Please bring sour cream and margarine on the side.
- May I have the rest of this wrapped to take home? (Actually, this is a great request for any restaurant.)
- May we share dinner and order an extra salad?

Eating out has become a common activity in our busy lives. Remember, it is not the last time you will be going out to eat. Choose wisely. It is essential you learn to take responsibility for your choices and exercise portion control. It **is** possible to eat out and lose weight!

Conclusion

Incorporate all meals into your daily exchanges. When eating out, we suggest ordering based on the following exchanges:

Lunch	**Dinner**
2-3 protein	3-4 protein
1 bread	2 bread
1 fat	2 fat
1 vegetable	1 vegetable

References:

Warshaw, Hope S. <u>The Restaurant Companion.</u> Surrey Books, 1990.

"Sam's" Brain. Sorry not a book yet, you need to pick it!

Fast Food Survival

An occasional meal at a fast food restaurant will not sabotage your healthy eating. There is hardly a fast food restaurant today that does not offer lean, low-fat choices.

Think, before you order. Do not order an item out of habit or because you are tempted by the aromas. That item could be loaded with fat, sodium and calories. Do not be fooled into thinking that fast food chains have become a multi-million dollar business because their food is so great or because they are fast. From the time you walk in the door you become a sale, just how big a sale depends on how well trained the staff is and how unaware you are.

How much time do you have before you are asked for your order after you step up to the counter? Ten or maybe twenty seconds? Good service, huh? Imagine yourself being pressured and quickly looking up at the board to place your order. What glares back at you? The small letters listing all the food items or the **BIG** colored picture of the "so-called" specials? Chances are you are in a hurry, hungry, and will order something you were not planning on and it will not fit into your exchanges for the day.

Therefore, decide what you will order *before* you enter the restaurant. After placing your order what is the next question you hear? "Would you like fries with that?" The sales person is NOT trying to be helpful, they are hoping to make a sale. Seventy five percent of all people will answer "yes" even if they had no intention of ordering fries. This is called "power of suggestion".

Most fast food restaurants now serve healthy salads, but we ruin the benefit of eating a salad with the dressing we drown it in. The typical high-fat dressing packet is **four** servings and has 350 to 390 calories per package! Is the nutritional information listed on the packet? Maybe not! It might be on the box all the packets came in. If it is high in calories, they certainly are not going to brag about it. The worst offenders are Thousand Island and Blue Cheese. Whatever you choose, it is best to choose one that is reduced in calories. Look for no more than 45 calories per serving which will equal one fat exchange.

One day I watched a customer order a salad and add two packages of high fat dressing and two packages of croutons. Croutons are fifty calories per packet which equals one bread exchange. I wanted to run right up to her and say, "hold it!" If she had ordered the fattest, sloppiest burger, she probably would have consumed less fat and calories! The salad was only 230 calories, but the dressing and croutons added 800 calories! But, of course, she was eating salad so in her mind it was a real sacrifice - she was "dieting!"

French fries are fine, but ten (that is 10) of them equal one high-fat bread. Can YOU eat just ten? In fact, if you order a medium order of fries you have enough carbohydrates and fat to equal two baked potatoes with two teaspoons of margarine. Would you eat two baked potatoes with your meal? Not likely.

Order sandwiches without mayonnaise. Most mayonnaise is added to a sandwich with a spatula or a squirt gun that serves 120 calories worth, or all three fat exchanges for the day. Bacon is fifty calories per slice and cheese is one hundred calories (80% of which is fat). So much for your bacon cheeseburger at 320 calories more than a plain hamburger with lettuce, tomato and onions. I didn't say DON'T use mayonnaise, however, you decide how much you want to use by ordering it on the side.

If you must order chicken at a fast food restaurant, order only the chicken breast. The thigh, drumstick and wing have more breading than meat. Breading absorbs more fat. A wing has nearly as many calories as a breast. There are occasions, such as picnics, when we cannot avoid the fried chicken. If you take off the skin you can save lots of calories. Think about what you are eating. Have you ever taken a look under the breading on a piece of chicken to see what is left on the skin? Yuk! Chickens today do not get plucked the way Grandma used to do it, and they probably do not get washed the same way either. Just what is that slimy stuff on the underside of the breading? To make chicken nuggets or strips the chicken is usually ground raw with the skin, fat and all. Next they are breaded and deep fried.

I cannot believe how people are fooled by breakfast at fast food restaurants. The average fast food Danish is 393 calories. This is one fourth of the day's calories if you are on 1200 calories per day! "But they are so small," you cry. It is NOT worth it! You could have had a 4 oz. sirloin, baked potato, salad, two fats and a vegetable, plus a beverage for the same number of calories in that small Danish. *Think before you act!* Very few fast food restaurants give you a choice of cereal and milk or a scrambled egg and a pancake for breakfast. Most fast food breakfasts are anywhere from 600 - 1000 calories, which is nearly a full day's calories.

Sensibly Thin Exchange Program

BONUS CALORIE CHOICES:

What are Bonus Calorie Choices? This is the fun food. (Far Out - Kool - Yea!) The food that probably led you to being overweight in the first place. (Oh!) Feeling deprived (wa, wa) can lead to an increased desire for food, and eventually to overeating. All foods you eat will be part of your daily diet. If this is going to be a lifelong change, it is very important that you learn to eat a wide variety and not overdo any one food. A healthier lifestyle is realizing that having a tasty morsel of sugar *occasionally* won't make you overweight again.

The suggested calorie level for a Bonus Calorie Choice is approximately 250 calories twice a week. 250 calories is a candy bar, an extra piece of cheese pizza, 6 pieces of light bread with fat or that small piece of cake at the party. If you are planning to go out and would enjoy having a glass of wine or that *small* dessert, these would be considered one of your two choices.

Sam's Note:
If you decide to eat more than 2 bonus choices per week think of yourself standing naked in front of a mirror chowing down. So, go ahead, enjoy those 6 cookies.

Weight loss plans that can't be adapted to the occasional treats or celebrations are headed for failure. There is no food you can't have. The *amount of food* and *how often* you are choosing it is the most important part of selecting your **Bonus Calorie** choices.

"I forget. Is carrot cake a vegetable?"

FRUIT: is a simple carbohydrate that is easy for the body to absorb and use. Fruits are packed with vitamins and minerals. Chocolate is a simple carbohydrate but is considered empty because it is so low in vitamins and minerals.

Use fresh fruits or fruits frozen or canned without sugar. The fruits with an asterisk next to them are high in natural sugar, therefore watch the amounts! The sweeter the fruit the less you get for an exchange.

1 Tbsp. honey or syrup may be exchanged for a fruit when used in a recipe, however, they do not contain the necessary Vitamin A and C so use them sparingly.

One fruit exchange equals the measurement given and provides 60 calories.
Women = 3 Exchanges
Men = 4 Exchanges

apple (1 medium)
apple juice (1/2 cup)
unsweetened applesauce (1/2 cup)
apricots, medium (4)
blueberries (3/4 cup)
*cherries (12)
cranberries, unsweetened as desired
cranberries, canned (2 Tbsp.)
dates (2)
figs (2)
grapefruit (1/2)
grapefruit juice (1/2 cup)
*grapes (15)
*grape juice (1/3 cup)
kiwi, large (1)

mango, small (1/2)
honeydew melon (1/8 melon)
cantaloupe (1/3 melon)
watermelon (1 1/4 cup)
melon, cubes (1 cup)
fresh mixed fruit (1 cup)
orange, medium (1)
orange juice (1/2 cup)
papaya (1 cup)
peach, medium (1)
pear, small (1)
pineapple (3/4 cup)
*pineapple juice (1/2 cup)
plums, medium (2)
prunes, medium (3)
prune juice (1/3 cup)
*raisins (2 Tbsp.)
raspberries (1 cup)
strawberries (1 cup)
tangerines, medium (2)
nectarine, medium (1)
Fruit canned in own juice (1/2 cup)
Fruit canned in light syrup (1/2 cup)
*banana small (1/2)

Try to eat 1 citrus fruit per day for the vitamin C. Many people wait until they have a cold to take Vitamin C. How about a little preventive medicine!

> **Sam's Note:**
> *I hate leaving a half a banana on the counter. So I buy small and eat the whole thing.*

VEGETABLES: are complex carbohydrates that produce long term energy for the body.

Almost always you can have unlimited vegetables as long as you are careful about what you put on them. You can exchange 6 oz. tomato juice or vegetable juice as a fruit or a vegetable.

One vegetable exchange equals 1/2 cup cooked or 1 cup raw and provides 25 calories.
Women = 2 Exchanges
Men = 2 Exchanges

artichoke, medium (1/2)
asparagus
beans, green or yellow
bean sprouts
beets
bell peppers, green or red
broccoli
brussels sprouts
cabbage
carrots
cauliflower
celery
cucumbers
eggplant
lettuce
mushrooms

onions
pea pods
radishes
rhubarb
rutabaga
sauerkraut
spinach
sprouts
summer squash
tomato (1 large)
tomato juice
turnips
vegetable juice
water chestnuts
zucchini

Sam's Note: It takes 3,500 extra calories in your diet to gain 1 pound of body fat. 1 cup raw or 1/2 cup cooked vegetables = 25 calories. I have never met anyone who gained a pound of body fat by eating too many vegetables. You would need to eat 140 cups of raw vegetables to equal 3,500 calories!!

MILK: helps us meet our calcium needs and also provides much needed protein and minerals.

One non-fat milk exchange equals the measurement given and provides 80-100 calories.
Women = 2 Exchanges
Men = 4 Exchanges

skim milk (1 cup)
non-fat dry milk (1/3 cup)
non-fat plain yogurt (8 oz.)
evaporated skim milk (1/2 cup)
low-fat buttermilk (1 cup)
sugar-free pudding (1/2 cup)
sugar-free hot cocoa (1 cup)
frozen yogurt (1/2 cup)
non-fat yogurt cone (100 cal.)
light ice cream (1/2 cup) **Measure! The lick on the spoon counts.**

Note: 1/2 cup Sherbet equals 1 bread exchange, sorry not enough calcium.

Exchanging light ice cream for a milk exchange should be done only **once a day,** since it does not have as much calcium as a glass of skim milk. Adults who are drinking only one milk exchange should try to use a calcium fortified milk. RDA recommends 800mg. of calcium per day.

BREAD: is a complex carbohydrate and more difficult for the body to absorb than simple carbohydrates. Therefore, they last longer. One ounce of a bread product, including rice, pasta and cereal is one exchange.

One bread exchange equals the measurement given and provides 80-100 calories. *High-fat bread exchanges contain up to 125 calories.
Women = 4 Exchanges
Men = 5 Exchanges

Bread
all light breads (40 calories for two slices)
light buns (whole) or regular buns (1/2)
white or whole wheat (1 slice)
raisin (1 slice)
French or Italian (1 slice)
pumpernickel (1 slice)
rye bread (1 slice)
Pita bread (1/2 large or whole small)
bagel, small, 2 oz. (1/2)
English muffin (1/2)
dinner roll (1)
tortilla (6 in.)
bread crumbs (2 Tbsp.)
flour (2 1/2 Tbsp.)
croutons (2 Tbsp.)
rice cakes (2 large)
popcorn cakes (70-80 calories)
sherbet (1/2 cup)
1 oz. angel food cake (not exactly the size Grandma used to cut)

Watch out for the salad bars. 2 Tbsp. croutons equals 1 bread exchange. Most of us think of croutons at a salad bar as being free. No more, the good life at the salad bar has ended!

Cereal
bran flakes (1/2 cup)
Grape Nuts (1/4 cup)
unfrosted puffed cereal (1 cup)
ready to eat unsweetened cereal (3/4 cup)

Cereal may be exchanged as a bread or as a protein if 1/2 cup milk is consumed at the same time. Check cereal box for serving size. Calories per serving should be close to 100. If it is not, reduce the serving size to come as close to 80-100 calories. Kids cereals usually contain a lot of sugar.

Cooked pasta
macaroni (1/2 cup)
spaghetti (1/2 cup)
pasta salad (1/2 cup)
rice (1/2 cup)

> *Sam's Note:*
> *Microwave popcorn is very high in fat and sodium. Some packages contain 3 or more servings. Look for light, and be sure to check the serving size.*

Crackers
pretzel sticks (25)
rye wafers (3)
graham (4 quarters, 2 halves, 1 sheet)
saltines (6) *2 are free once a day*
oyster (20) round or butter type (5)

Beans, Peas & Lentils (1/2 cup)
kidney beans (1/2 cup)
baked beans, no pork (1/4 cup)
fat-free refried beans (1/2 cup) regular (1/4 cup)

Starchy Vegetables
peas, corn (1/2 cup)
lima beans (1/2 cup)
corn on the cob (small)
potato (4 oz.) mashed potato (1/2 cup)
pumpkin (3/4 cup)
sweet potato (1/3 cup)
winter squash (1 cup)
potato salad (1/2 cup)

Sam's Note:
We grew up thinking of corn and peas as just a vegetable, so what gives? They contain more starch which converts to sugar making them high enough in calories to be counted as a bread. 60 calories per serving.

*High-Fat Breads: are like putting margarine on bread, 80 calories for the bread and 45 calories for the fat totaling **125 calories. Limit yourself to 1 High-fat bread per day.**

corn bread (2 oz.)
pancake (size of a piece of bread)
waffle (size of a piece of bread)
round 4 section Belgium waffle = 8 breads
muffin (1 oz.)
BIG 8 oz. muffins can be up to 8 High Fat breads!
French fries (10)
Potato or corn chips (10) Count out and put them in front of you before you begin to eat.

Sam's Note:
Serve syrup on the side and dip each bite into the syrup or dip your fork tines into the syrup and then take a bite of pancake or waffle. Twice the flavor, half the calories.

FATS: provide three things. 1. Insulation which most of us already have plenty of. 2. They help to transport vitamins and minerals throughout the body. 3. Fat helps cushion the body to prevent bones from breaking. Only 30-35% of all daily calories should come from fat. Don't forget all the foods that have hidden fats. Measure fats carefully because they are high in calories.

One fat exchange equals the measurement given and provides 45 calories.
Women = 3 Exchanges
Men = 3 Exchanges

Unsaturated fats remain soft at room temperature.
margarine (1 tsp.)
margarine, diet
mayonnaise (1 tsp.)
mayonnaise, reduced calorie (1 Tbsp.)
Miracle Whip (2 tsp.)
Miracle Whip Light (1 Tbsp.)
salad dressing, all varieties (1 Tbsp.)
salad dressing, all varieties, reduced calorie (2 Tbsp.)
oil: corn, safflower, olive and peanut (1 tsp.)
peanut butter (1 1/2 tsp.)
black or green olives (10 small) or (5 large)
avocado, medium (1/8)

Sam's Note:
I yi yi - If 1/8 of an avocado is a fat exchange at 50 calories, then imagine mixing it with mayonnaise for guacamole! 1/4 cup is 200 calories.

Sam's Note:
When eating salad dressing, dip the tines of the fork into the dressing and then take a bite of salad. Half the calories, twice the taste.

If you choose to use reduced calorie fats, read the label. One fat exchange equals 45 calories. There are 9 calories per gram of fat. 5 x 9 = 45 calories or 5 grams of fat.

Nuts, you are nuts to eat nuts.
Almonds (6) sliced or slivered (1 tsp.)
pecans (2)
cashews (2)
peanuts (10) dry roasted, honey roasted, Spanish (20)
sunflower seeds (1 Tbsp.) in the shell (2 Tbsp.)
walnuts (2)

Saturated fats stay solid at room temperature.
butter (1 tsp.)
bacon (1 strip)
coconut (2 Tbsp.)
light cream cheese (1 Tbsp.)
cream, heavy (1 Tbsp.)
cream, light (2 Tbsp.)
sour cream (2 Tbsp.)
gravy (1 Tbsp.)
real bacon pieces (2 Tbsp. = 1 protein)
Avoid palm and coconut oil.

Sam's Note:
When eating a BLT, count one strip of bacon as one protein exchange. Any other time, bacon is a fat exchange. (This gives you a little flexibility so your fats won't all be used on a single sandwich.)

LEAN PROTEIN: We want to be sure to get enough protein so the body does not take protein from its own muscle. Proteins play an important job that many other foods can not do alone. The more often you choose from this group versus the medium-fat and high-fat groups, the faster your weight loss will be.

One lean protein exchange equals 1 oz. of a cooked meat and/or provides 55 calories.
Women = 6 Exchanges
Men = 8 Exchanges

Beef
flank steak
chipped beef
top & bottom round
sirloin
rump roast
tenderloin
eye of round
filet mignon without bacon wrap

Pork
ham, center cut (deli shaved or sliced)
pork tenderloin
Canadian bacon

Lamb & Veal
loin and sirloin
leg of lamb

Poultry, remove skin before cooking.
chicken **30 calories per oz.**
turkey **40 calories per oz.**
turkey hot dog **30 calories per oz.**

Fish

fresh and frozen (1 oz.)
canned salmon (1/4 cup)
tuna (1/4 cup)
crab (1/4 cup)
lobster (1/4 cup)
sardines (3)

Sam's Note:
Yuck! Did you know they don't usually filet them and remove the innards from sardines?

Sam's Note:
Salmon is naturally higher in oil at 40 calories per oz. Big deal compared to what? It's still good for you.

Cheese

cheese of 55 or fewer calories per oz.
ricotta, part-skim (1/4 cup)
fat-free cream cheese
fat-free and 1% cottage cheese (1/4 cup)

Sam's Note:
There are a lot of low-calorie cheeses on the market today. Be sure to look for them. Fat-free does not melt, but softens. It is perfect for grilled hamburger, pizza, and sandwiches.

Beans, Peas & Lentils (1/2 cup)
kidney beans (1/2 cup)
baked beans, no pork (1/4 cup)
fat-free refried beans (1/2 cup) regular (1/4 cup)

Wild Game
most wild game is a lean protein exchange

Other
light or lean luncheon meat (less than 10% fat)
egg substitutes (1/4 cup = 1 protein)

MEDIUM-FAT PROTEIN: When choosing from this group, please keep in mind that you are consuming 20 calories more per ounce than if you were choosing from the lean protein group. Limit foods from this group to **two main meals per week.**

One medium-fat exchange equals 1 oz. of a cooked meat and/or provides 75 calories.
Women = 6 Exchanges
Men = 8 Exchanges

Beef
ground beef (no more than 10% fat)
rib eye steak
cubed steak
T-bone steak
meat loaf
porterhouse steak
ground round

Pork
lean chops

Poultry
domestic duck/goose (well drained of fat)
ground turkey (no more than 10% fat)

Sam's Note:
Remember when making a recipe with ground turkey be sure to pick a package that states no more than 10% fat, or you may end up with the eyes, neck, beak and feathers!

Cheese
cheese that is 80 calories or less per oz.
look for part-skim (i.e. mozzarella, ricotta, Farmer's)
Parmesan (2 Tbsp.)
Neufchatel (light cream cheese)
2% cottage cheese (1/4 cup)

Organ Meats
heart
liver
kidneys

Sam's Note:
If you are watching your cholesterol, try to avoid
eating a lot of organ meats.

Other
eggs, limit to 3 per week because of cholesterol
Try a 2 egg omelet.

HIGH-FAT PROTEIN: When choosing from this group, please keep in mind that you are consuming 45 more calories per ounce than if you were choosing from the lean protein group. Limit foods from this group to <u>one main meal per week.</u>

One high-fat protein exchange equals 1 oz. of a cooked meat and/or provides 100 calories.
Women = 6 Exchanges
Men = 8 Exchanges

Beef
ground chuck (comes from chuck roast)
rib steak
ground beef (more than 20% fat)

Pork
spare ribs
deviled ham
country-style ham
ground pork
sausage (more than 10% fat)

Lamb & Veal
breast

Cheese
all cheese that are 100-110 calories per oz. (i.e. American, Cheddar, Swiss, Monterey Jack, Colby, and CoJack)

Other
luncheon meats (more than 5% fat)
sausage (polish, Italian)
bratwurst, hot dogs
peanut butter (1 Tbsp.)

MISCELANEOUS

Some of you may have used an exchange program in the past. We think you will find the **SENSIBLY THIN** application of the exchange program is easier and more livable.

A standard exchange plan requires that you calculate the breads, proteins, vegetables, fats, etc., that are components of soups and casseroles. We simplify this using the following:

meat based casseroles, spaghetti, chili, beef stew, and chow mein without noodles or rice
1/4 cup = 1 protein

soup, broth based (vegetable, chicken noodle, tomato made with water, etc.)
1 cup = 1 protein

soup, milk base (clam chowder, cream of broccoli, etc.)
1 cup = 2 protein Don't push it. Most milk based soups are cream based. Some creamed soups can be as high as 500 calories per cup.

Pizza; cheese, Canadian bacon & vegetable pizza
2 slices = 2 bread and 3 protein

Sam's Note:
Consider this a gift once a week and don't abuse this. Plain cheese pizza is 330 calories per slice. If you ate 3 pieces, image what that could do to a 1200 calorie day!

Free Foods

As always, **nothing** in life is free! Please use portion control.

tonic water, sugar-free
drink mixes, sugar-free
gelatin, sugar-free
gum (sugar-free is best for your teeth)
jam or jelly (1 tsp.) this is great on your 2 free saltines
pancake syrup, sugar-free (2 Tbsp.)
whipped topping (2 Tbsp.)
ketchup and mustard (1 Tbsp.)
taco sauce (1 Tbsp.)
cocktail sauce (1 Tbsp.)
bouillon or broth

We do strongly suggest that you consult your physician for approval of our plan if it differs greatly from a diet that you have already received under medical supervision.

How to Plan a Menu

1. Choose what you will eat for your main meal.
   Working from that meal will make it easier to plan the
   rest of the day.

2. Decide which meat you want to prepare and which
   recipe you will use.

3. Fill in your menu plan as you eat each meal and snack
   to record accurately what you have eaten in one day.

4. Make out your grocery list at the same time as the menu
   plan is made.

5. **Don't skip any foods.** You will only sabotage yourself.

6. Keep your menu varied and interesting.

Abbreviations for Exchanges

P	Lean Protein	55 calories or less per oz.
MFP	Medium Fat Protein	75 calories per oz.
HFP	High Fat Protein	100 plus calories per oz.
B	Bread	80-100 calories per oz.
HFB	High Fat Bread	80+45=125 calories per oz.
M	Milk	80-100 calories per serving
Fr	Fruit	60 calories per serving
F	Fat	45 calories per serving
V	Vegetable	25 calories per serving

SENSIBLY THIN®

"All things are possible to those who believe"

Behavior Change/Goal For Week _____

Questions For Class _____

© Copyright 1992

Day:							
Breakfast 1 protein 1 bread 1/2 c. milk							
10:00 fruit							
Lunch 2 protein 1 bread 1 fat 1 vegetable 1 milk							
3:00 fruit							
Dinner 3 protein 1 bread 2 fat 1 vegetable 1/2 c. milk							
8:00 planned snack							
fruit	☐ ☐	☐ ☐	☐ ☐	☐ ☐	☐ ☐	☐ ☐	☐ ☐
vegetable	☐ ☐	☐ ☐	☐ ☐	☐ ☐	☐ ☐	☐ ☐	☐ ☐
milk	☐ ☐	☐ ☐	☐ ☐	☐ ☐	☐ ☐	☐ ☐	☐ ☐
bread	☐ ☐ (☐)	☐ ☐ (☐)	☐ ☐ (☐)	☐ ☐ (☐)	☐ ☐ (☐)	☐ ☐ (☐)	☐ ☐ (☐)
fat	☐ ☐	☐ ☐	☐ ☐	☐ ☐	☐ ☐	☐ ☐	☐ ☐
protein	☐ ☐ ☐ ☐ ☐ ☐	☐ ☐ ☐ ☐ ☐ ☐	☐ ☐ ☐ ☐ ☐ ☐	☐ ☐ ☐ ☐ ☐ ☐	☐ ☐ ☐ ☐ ☐ ☐	☐ ☐ ☐ ☐ ☐ ☐	☐ ☐ ☐ ☐ ☐ ☐
water	☐ ☐ ☐ ☐ ☐ ☐ ☐ ☐	☐ ☐ ☐ ☐ ☐ ☐ ☐ ☐	☐ ☐ ☐ ☐ ☐ ☐ ☐ ☐	☐ ☐ ☐ ☐ ☐ ☐ ☐ ☐	☐ ☐ ☐ ☐ ☐ ☐ ☐ ☐	☐ ☐ ☐ ☐ ☐ ☐ ☐ ☐	☐ ☐ ☐ ☐ ☐ ☐ ☐ ☐
Exercise 30 min minimum 3x							
Bonus Calories 2x							
Excess Foods							
Comments Re: Day							

SENSIBLY THIN

Mens

"All things are possible to those who believe"

© Copyright 1992

Behavior Change/Goal For Week _____

Questions For Class _____

Day:							
Breakfast 2 protein / 1 bread / 1 c. milk							
10:00 fruit							
Lunch 2 protein / 2 bread / 1 fat / 1 vegetable / 1 milk							
3:00 fruit							
Dinner 4 protein / 2 bread / 2 fat / 1 vegetable / 1 c. milk							
8:00 planned snack							
fruit							
vegetable							
milk							
bread							
fat							
protein							
water							
Exercise 30 min minimum 3x							
Bonus Calories 2x							
Excess Foods							
Comments Re: Day							

xlvii

Changing Behaviors

Becoming AWARE of why and where you are overeating is an essential part of the success of a permanent weight-loss plan. Each week we ask that you choose a behavior to work on. Until the behavior has changed, the weight loss won't be permanent. Start by identifying the behaviors that got you in trouble with your eating. Can you identify with some of the behaviors expressed below? Continue weekly to add a new behavior change to replace the old behaviors.

This week I shall try changing this behavior:

- I will eat breakfast to start my furnace (burning calories by eating breakfast). By doing this, I will lose more weight than by getting too hungry and snacking later.

- I will eat only in the kitchen while sitting at a table. It is easy to consume an extra 500 calories while snacking, standing or watching TV.

- I will drink water before I eat. It will help me to feel more full and, therefore, I will eat less.

- I will eat slowly and enjoy my food thoroughly.

- I will use a smaller plate because it makes my portions appear larger.

- I will stop and not eat more because I think I am still hungry. I will wait 20 minutes since it usually takes that long for my stomach to tell my brain that

I'm full.

- I will not eat fried foods because frying can triple the calories.

- I will buy my favorite tempting foods in small individual size packages for automatic portion control.

- I will brush my teeth after each meal. A clean fresh mouth is enough to discourage continuous eating.

- I will offer myself non-food rewards for each weight-loss goal. Losing weight is an accomplishment. It's something worth celebrating!

- I will chew sugarless gum while preparing dinner. It will help me to control my nibbling.

- I will eat three meals per day with nutritious snacks included throughout the day. By doing this, I will not be so hungry. This will also prevent my overeating at the next meal. Instead of becoming too hungry before going out to dinner, I will have fruit or a cup of sugar-free hot cocoa. These few calories will save me hundreds.

- If my family insists on eating junk food, I will ask them not to eat it in front of me, out of sight, out of mind.

- When I lose weight, I will have my clothes altered or I will give them away. I will not keep them, "just in case."

And remember, if nothing changes, nothing changes.

Breakfast Patties

1 medium onion, finely chopped
1 apple, pared and shredded
1 lb. ground turkey (no more than 10% fat)
1 tsp. dried thyme
1 tsp. fennel seeds, crushed
1/2 tsp. ground allspice
1/4 tsp. pepper
ground nutmeg, pinch

- In microwave, cook onion and apple for 1 minute.

- Combine all ingredients.

- Divide and shape into 6 round patties.

- Cook patties over medium heat in non-stick skillet,
  3 minutes per side. (Turkey does not brown like
  high-fat sausage. It will remain light colored.)

- Uncooked patties can be frozen. When cooking frozen
  patties, fry 5 minutes per side.

Submitted by Carol Dobitz
Serves 6   **Serv/Size** 1 patty   **Cal/Serv** 100   **Sodium** 40mg
Cholesterol 45mg   **Fiber** trace   **Fat/Serv** trace   **Fat** 5%

Exchanges: 2P

Sam's Meal Ideas:
Serve with chive-scrambled eggs and apple wedges.

Turkey Patty

1 lb. ground turkey (no more than 10% fat)
1/4 tsp. ground sage
1/2 tsp. fennel seed
1/2 tsp. Italian seasoning
1 tsp. salt
1/4 tsp. pepper

- Combine above ingredients, shape into 6 patties.

- Cook patties over medium heat in non-stick skillet, 3 minutes per side. (Turkey does not brown like high-fat sausage. It will remain light colored.)

Submitted by Mary Lynk
Serves 6   Serv/Size 1 patty   **Cal/Serv** 80   **Sodium** 420mg
Cholesterol 45mg   **Fiber** 0g   **Fat/Serv** 0g   **Fat** 6%

Exchanges: 2P

Sam's Note:
Shop around for ground turkey as you would ground beef. The package may say 100% turkey, but keep in mind the skin and fat from turkey are also 100% turkey. Buy no more than 10% fat. To be sure you are getting pure ground turkey, ask your butcher to grind a one pound turkey breast for you.

Egg Beaters

4 egg whites
1 tsp. vegetable oil
2 drops yellow food coloring

● Mix together and shake vigorously.

Serves 2   **Serv/Size** 1/2   **Cal/Serv** 50   **Sodium** 110mg
Cholesterol 0mg   **Fiber** 0g   **Fat/Serv** 2g   **Fat** 40%

Exchanges: 1P

Sam's Note:
This egg beater recipe is a lot less expensive than buying egg substitute cartons in the grocery store. The original egg beater recipe called for 1 Tbsp. oil. I made the recipe using only 1 tsp. oil and the eggs were delicious! A little oil is necessary or the eggs will be hard. A large egg with yolk is 80 calories and 280mg of cholesterol, a significant difference.

Eggs Florentine

1 pkg. (10 oz.) frozen spinach
4 tomato slices
4 eggs, poached
2 whole English muffins (toasted)
paprika
Tarragon Sauce:
1/3 cup non-fat mayonnaise
2 Tbsp. water
2 tsp. lemon juice
3/4 tsp. mustard
1/8 tsp. tarragon
dash pepper

- Prepare tarragon sauce, cook over low heat 3 minutes until warm. Do not boil.
- Cook spinach, drain.
- Place equal amounts of spinach and a tomato slice on each half of toasted muffins.
- Top with egg, spoon 2 Tbsp. tarragon sauce over each muffin.
- Sprinkle with paprika.

Serves 4   **Serv/Size** 1/2 English muffin   **Cal/Serv** 180
Sodium 540mg   **Calcium** 150mg   **Cholesterol** 200mg
Fiber 3.5g   **Fat/Serv** 6g   **Fat** 30%

Exchanges: 1P, 1B

Sam's Note:
If this recipe is used for brunch, you could serve each person both halves of the English muffin. Garnish with fresh fruit. Exchanges would then be 2P, 2B, 1F.

New Mexico Scrambled Eggs

5 eggs and 3 egg whites
1/2 cup water
1/2 tsp. salt
1/8 tsp. pepper
1/2 tsp. parsley
1 small tomato, chopped
2 green onions, finely chopped
salsa (optional)

- Preheat oven to 350°.

- Beat eggs and water together. Mix in remaining ingredients.

- Place in an 8x8" baking dish coated with non-stick spray.

- Bake covered 20 minutes.

- Top with salsa.

Serves 4   **Serv/Size** 1/4   **Cal/Serv** 116   **Sodium** 400mg
Cholesterol 265mg   **Fiber** 0g   **Fat/Serv** 6g   **Fat** 50%

Exchanges: 2P

Egg Casserole

1 lb. ground turkey (no more than 10% fat)
8 slices light bread, cubed (40 calories per slice)
2 cups (8 oz.) light Cheddar cheese, shredded
2 eggs and 4 egg whites
1 cup skim milk (calcium fortified)
1 can (10.75 oz.) low-fat cream of mushroom soup
parsley
paprika
Mix ground turkey with:
1 tsp. garlic powder
1 tsp. Italian seasoning
1/2 tsp. fennel seed

- Preheat oven to 350°.
- Brown turkey, drain.
- Place bread cubes in bottom of a 7x11" baking dish coated with non-stick spray.
- Add turkey and cheese.
- Beat eggs, add milk and soup, blend. Pour over turkey, refrigerate overnight.
- Bake covered 1 hour.
- Top with fresh parsley and paprika.

Submitted by Sam
Serves 6   **Serv/Size** 1/8   **Cal/Serv** 286   **Sodium** 1072mg
Calcium 325mg   **Cholesterol** 160mg   **Fiber** 3g
Fat/Serv 7g   **Fat** 25%

Exchanges: 3P, 2B

Sausage Brunch

1 lb. breakfast sausage (i.e. Jimmy Dean)
2 cups stuffing mix
2 cups (8 oz.) light Cheddar cheese, shredded
2 eggs and 2 egg whites
3/4 tsp. dry mustard
1 1/2 cups skim milk (calcium fortified)
1 can (10.75 oz.) low-fat cream of mushroom soup
1/2 cup skim milk (calcium fortified)

- Preheat oven to 350°.
- Brown sausage, drain.
- Place stuffing mix on bottom of a 9x13" baking dish coated with non-stick spray.
- Top stuffing with sausage and cheese.
- Beat eggs, mustard and milk. Pour over sausage.
- Cover with foil, refrigerate overnight.
- Mix soup and remaining milk, pour over casserole.
- Bake covered 1 hour.

Submitted by Mike Unhjem
Serves 10　**Serv/Size** one piece　**Cal/Serv** 275
Sodium 930mg　**Calcium** 243mg　**Cholesterol** 75mg
Fiber 1g　**Fat/Serv** 17g　**Fat** 56%

Exchanges: 2P, 1B (This is a high fat protein, not lean, not medium, we said high fat!!!!!)

Sam's Note: I made this 10 servings rather than 8 because of the percentage of fat. Better to serve smaller and serve a fat-free muffin with fresh fruit. Be sure to use stuffing mix NOT croutons. Stuffing is fat free. Croutons are very high in fat.

Naturally Slim Quiche

9" unbaked pie shell
1 egg white, slightly beaten
1/2 jar (2 oz.) real bacon pieces
2 cups (8 oz.) Swiss cheese, shredded
2 eggs and 2 egg whites
1 cup skim milk (calcium fortified)
1/4 tsp. salt
1/8 tsp. nutmeg
dash pepper

- Preheat oven to 350°.
- Brush inside of pie shell with egg white, refrigerate 10 minutes.
- Sprinkle bacon and cheese in bottom of shell.
- Beat together rest of ingredients, slowly pour into pie shell.
- Move oven rack to lowest position.
- Bake 40 minutes until golden or knife inserted in middle comes out clean.
- Cool 10 minutes, to allow eggs to set, before serving.

Serves 6 **Serv/Size** 1/6 **Cal/Serv** 350
Sodium 535mg **Calcium** 513mg **Cholesterol** 110mg
Fiber trace **Fat/Serv** 20g **Fat** 50%

Exchanges: 2P, 1HFB

Sam's Note:
HFB (high fat bread) is equal to one slice of bread with 1 tsp. margarine. 80 calories plus 45 calories=125

Spinach Quiche

1 egg white, lightly beaten
9" unbaked pie shell
1/2 cup onion, chopped
1 pkg. (10 oz.) frozen spinach, chopped
2 Tbsp. parsley, chopped
2 eggs and 2 egg whites
1 cup skim milk (calcium fortified)
1/8 tsp. nutmeg (optional)
1/4 tsp. salt
dash pepper
2 cups (8 oz.) Swiss cheese, shredded

- Preheat oven to 350°.
- Brush inside of pie shell with egg white, refrigerate 10 minutes.
- Sauté onion 1 minute in microwave.
- Thaw and squeeze frozen spinach to remove water, mix in onion and parsley. Microwave on high 1 minute, cool.
- Whisk together rest of ingredients, except cheese. Add to **cooled** spinach so egg will not cook.
- Sprinkle cheese over bottom of cooled crust. Top with spinach mixture.
- Bake 50 minutes, or until set in center.

Submitted by Sam
Serves 6   **Serv/Size** 1/6   **Cal/Serv** 250   **Calcium** 574mg
Sodium 450mg   **Cholesterol** 105mg   **Fiber** 2.5g
Fat/Serv 19g   **Fat** 48%

Exchanges: 2P, 1HFB, 1V

Sam's Note:
Quiche is done when knife inserted in center comes out clean.

Asparagus Strata

12 slices light bread (40 calories per slice)
1 cup (4 oz.) low-fat Cheddar cheese, shredded
1 lb. fresh asparagus
8 oz. (1 1/2 cups) cooked ham, diced
3 eggs and 3 egg whites, beaten
3 cups skim milk (calcium fortified)
1/2 cup onion, finely chopped
1/2 tsp. dry mustard
1/2 tsp. salt
1/4 tsp. pepper
1/4 tsp. paprika

- Preheat oven to 350°.
- Using a glass turned upside down, press glass into center of bread to remove a 3" circle. Set circles aside. Tear remaining bread in small pieces, place in bottom of a 9x13" baking dish coated with non-stick spray.
- Cut asparagus in 1" pieces, microwave on high 3 minutes. Cool asparagus for a few minutes.
- On top of bread in dish, place cheese, asparagus, and ham. Top with bread circles.
- Combine all remaining ingredients, except paprika. Slowly pour egg mixture over bread circles.
- Sprinkle with paprika. Cover, chill 6 hours or overnight.
- Bake covered 40 minutes.

Submitted by Idella Wilson
Serves 8 **Serv/Size** 1/8 **Cal/Serv** 215 **Sodium** 944mg
Calcium 380mg **Cholesterol** 94mg **Fiber** 4g
Fat/Serv 6g **Fat** 24%

Exchanges: 3P, 1B

French Toast

4 eggs
1 1/2 cups skim milk (calcium fortified)
1/8 tsp. nutmeg
1 Tbsp. sugar
8 slices light (40 calories per slice) **or** regular bread

- Mix all ingredients.

- Coat non-stick skillet with cooking spray.

- Dip a slice of bread into egg mixture.

- Fry bread on both sides until golden brown.

- Mixture may be refrigerated up to 3 days.

Serves 4   **Serv/Size** 2 slices   **Cal/Serv** 125
Sodium 285mg   **Calcium** 213mg   **Cholesterol** 214mg
Fiber 4g   **Fat/Serv** 6g   **Fat** 29%

Exchanges: 2 slices light bread=1P,   1B
**   2 slices regular bread=1P,   2B**

Sam's Note:
Dip the tines of the fork into syrup first. Twice the sweetness and 1/2 the calories! Read the label on syrup. Syrups vary from 4 calories in sugar-free up to 50 calories per tablespoon in regular syrup. 50 Calories=1 fruit! No vitamin A or C is provided.

Artichoke Dip

1 can (14 oz.) artichoke hearts
1/2 cup Parmesan cheese, grated
1/2 cup (2 oz.) part-skim Mozzarella cheese, shredded
1/2 cup light mayonnaise
1 tsp. garlic powder
1 Tbsp. green onion, chopped
1 can (4 oz.) chopped green chilies, drained, divided

- Preheat oven to 350°.

- Combine all ingredients, bake uncovered for 25 minutes in 1 1/2 quart casserole.

- Serve hot with crackers, or thinly sliced French or cocktail bread.

Serves 10   **Serv/Size** 1/3 cup   **Cal/Serv** 95
Sodium 220mg   **Calcium** 110mg   **Cholesterol** 10mg
Fiber trace   **Fat/Serv** 6g   **Fat** 58%

Exchanges: 1V, 1F

Sam's Note:
Green chilies come in a 4 oz. can. Use one-half can in this recipe and save the other half for a Mexican dish, or freeze the chilies for a later time.

Spinach Dip

1 pkg. (10 oz.) frozen chopped spinach
1 cup Miracle Whip Light
1/2 cup plain non-fat yogurt
1/2 cup light sour cream
1 can (8 oz.) sliced water chestnuts, drained and diced
1 pkg. (1.4 oz.) Knorr's vegetable soup mix
1 small onion, finely diced

- Thaw spinach, squeeze dry.

- Mix with all ingredients.

- Remove the top from a loaf of pumpernickel, french or rye bread. Hollow out bread, fill with dip.

- Cut remaining bread in cubes, place around loaf to use for dip.

Serves 12 **Serv/Size** 1/3 cup **Cal/Serv** 90
Sodium 200mg **Cholesterol** 10mg **Fiber** trace
Fat/Serv 7g **Fat** 70%

Exchanges: 2F

Sam's Note:
*Let's call a spade a spade! This dip is delicious and light, but it is still **2 fats for 1/3 cup**. Be sure to measure!*

Sam's Yogurt Dip

1 container (8 oz.) non-fat yogurt
2 Tbsp. light sour cream (optional)
1 pkg. (.4 oz) **or** 1/2 pkg. (1.1 oz.) dry ranch salad dressing
or any dry seasoning mix

- Mix ingredients together and enjoy.

Serves 4   **Serv/Size** 1/4 cup   **Cal/Serv** 30
Sodium 605mg   **Calcium** 110mg   **Cholesterol** 2mg
Fiber 0g   **Fat/Serv** 0g   **Fat** 12%

Exchanges: FREE!
        1/2 cup = 1/2M

Sam's Note:
Watch the package size on all ranch dressings. It comes in 2 sizes, .4 oz. and 1.1 oz. If you have the larger size, be sure and use only half. This recipe is also great on baked potatoes!!!

Skinny Spices

1 Tbsp. savory, crushed
1 Tbsp. thyme, crushed
1 Tbsp. fennel seeds
1 Tbsp. sage, crushed

1 Tbsp. marjoram, crushed
1 bay leaf, crushed
1/2 Tbsp. chives, chopped
1 Tbsp. dehydrated minced onion

- Combine all ingredients, store in airtight container. Use with following recipe, or in place of no-salt seasoning.

Submitted by Patty Ryland

Exchanges: FREE!

Skinny Spices Light Sauce

1/2 cup fat-free liquid margarine
2 tsp. grated lemon rind
3 Tbsp. lemon juice
1 Tbsp. Skinny Spices

- Combine all ingredients for an easy light sauce to accompany a fish entree. **This is great for grilled salmon.**

Submitted by Patty Ryland
Serves 2   Serv/Size 1/4 cup   Cal/Serv 30
Sodium 500mg   Cholesterol 0mg   Fiber 0g
Fat/Serv 0g   Fat 4%

Exchanges: FREE!

Parmesan Dressing

1 cup buttermilk
1 cup fat-free mayonnaise
1/3 cup fresh Parmesan cheese, grated
1 tsp. garlic powder
1/4 tsp. paprika
1/4 tsp. turmeric

- Combine ingredients, blend.

- Refrigerate covered, several hours or overnight.

Submitted by Patty Ryland
Serves 12   **Serving Size** 1 1/2 Tbsp.   **Cal/Serv** 32
Sodium 222mg   **Calcium** 55mg   **Cholesterol** 2mg
Fiber 0g   **Fat/Serv** 0g   **Fat** 25%

Exchanges: 1F

Sam's Note:
Well, it really is not a fat. But how do you count the calories? If you don't have buttermilk, add 1 Tbsp. vinegar or 1 Tbsp. lemon juice to 1 cup skim milk. Let milk stand five minutes.

The Most Wonderful Fruit Dip In The World

1 container (8 oz.) plain non-fat yogurt
1 container (8 oz.) fat-free cream cheese
4 pkts. Equal
1 tsp. vanilla **or** almond extract
1 tsp. lemon juice

- Blend and refrigerate.

Serves 4   **Serv/Size** 1/4 cup   **Cal/Serv** 100
Sodium 300mg   **Calcium** 115mg   **Cholesterol** 0mg
Fiber 0g   **Fat/Serv** 0g   **Fat** 0%

Exchanges: 1P

Snappy Fruit Dip

1 container (8 oz.) plain non-fat yogurt
1/2 cup light sour cream
1 Tbsp. honey
1 tsp. ginger

- Combine all ingredients, refrigerate.

- Serve your favorite fresh fruit arranged on a plate around a bowl of dip.

Submitted by Delores Tritten
Serves 4   **Serv/Size** 1/4 cup   **Cal/Serv** 80
Sodium 60mg   **Calcium** 115mg   **Cholesterol** 10mg
Fiber 0g   **Fat/Serv** 2g   **Fat** 20%

Exchanges: 1/2Fr,   1/2F

Mexican Cheese Dip

1 carton (8 oz.) plain non-fat yogurt
1/2 cup non-fat cottage cheese
1 garlic clove, minced
1 can (4 oz.) chopped green chilies, divided
1 tsp. chili powder
1/8 tsp. pepper

- Combine all ingredients.
- Cover, refrigerate about 1 hour.
- Stir before serving.
- Serve with assorted fresh vegetables.

Serves 4   **Serv/Size** 3 Tbsp.   **Cal/Serv** 55
Sodium 155mg   **Calcium** 120mg   **Cholesterol** 1mg
Fiber 0g   **Fat/Serv** 0g   **Fat** 2%

Exchanges: 1P

Sam's Note:
You could use the other half can of green chilies in any
Mexican recipe. ***Remember 10 chips = 1HFB.***

Sam's Meal Ideas:
*Have you tried the **Taco Casserole?** Serve the*
Mexican Cheese Dip and Taco Casserole together,
along with shredded lettuce, diced tomato, shredded
cheese on the same plate for color. Use salsa for
salad dressing. Both recipes serve four.

Sam's Salsa

1 can (16 oz.) tomatoes, peeled and diced
1/2 tsp. garlic powder
1/2 tsp. onion powder
3 pkts. Equal
1 1/2 tsp. cayenne (crushed red pepper)
2 tsp. cumin powder
2 tsp. cumin seeds

● Mix all together.

Submitted by Sam
Serves 4   Serv/Size 1/2 cup   **Cal/Serv** 40
Sodium 435mg   **Cholesterol** 0mg   **Fiber** 0g
Fat/Serv 0g   **Fat** 17%

Exchanges: 1V

Crab Cheese Ball

1 pkg. (8 oz.) light cream cheese
6 mock crab sticks, shredded
3 Tbsp. green onion, finely chopped
2 Tbsp. lemon juice
parsley

● Heat cream cheese in microwave on high 1 minute to soften.

● Add remaining ingredients, mix until blended.

● Chill slightly so cheese doesn't stick to hands. Form into small cheese ball. Garnish with parsley.

Serves 8   **Serv/Size** 3 Tbsp.   **Cal/Serv** 75
Sodium 240mg   **Calcium** 60mg   **Cholesterol** 50mg
Fiber 0g   **Fat/Serv** 9g   **Fat** 65%

Exchanges: 1F

Crab Spread

1 container (8 oz.) fat-free cream cheese, softened
20 mock crab sticks, cut up
3 green onions, diced with greens
1/2 green pepper, finely diced
1/2 cup cocktail sauce

- Mix together.

Submitted by Carol Dobitz
Serves 6   **Serv/Size** 1/2 cup   **Cal/Serv** 120
Sodium 585mg   **Calcium** 70mg   **Cholesterol** 35mg
Fiber trace   **Fat/Serv** 0g   **Fat** 0%

Exchanges: 2P

Sam's Note:
If you do not have cocktail sauce on hand, mix together
1/2 cup ketchup and horseradish to taste.
Serve this recipe with Wheat Thins.
12 crackers = 1 Bread exchange, 80 calories.

Chipped Beef Spread

1 container (8 oz.) fat-free cream cheese, softened
2 Tbsp. skim milk
1 pkg. (2 oz.) dried beef, cut up
2 Tbsp. green onion, minced
2 Tbsp. green pepper, minced
1/8 tsp. pepper
1/4 cup light sour cream
1/4 cup parsley

- Preheat oven to 350°.
- Blend cream cheese and milk.
- Add all ingredients, except parsley.
- Spread in bottom of glass pie pan. Sprinkle with parsley.
- Bake 15 minutes.
- Leftovers can be reheated in microwave.

Submitted by Carol Dobitz
Serves 6   Serv/Size 2 1/2 Tbsp.   Cal/Serv 80
Sodium 525mg   Cholesterol 10mg   Fiber trace
Fat/Serv 1g   Fat 12%

Exchanges: 1/2P,   1/2B

Sam Suggests:
Serve spread with rye or pumpernickel crackers, or cocktail bread. **6 crackers or 2 pieces of cocktail bread = 1 Bread exchange.**

Provolone Rounds

12 slices rye cocktail bread
1 Tbsp. margarine, softened
2 tsp. chives, dried
1/2 tsp. oregano
6 slices (1 oz. per slice) Provolone cheese, cut in half
6 cherry tomatoes, cut in half

- Cut Provolone halves in 2" round circles, an upside down juice glass works well.

- Combine margarine, chives, and oregano; spread on bread.

- Place bread on baking sheet, toast under broiler until lightly browned, 1 to 2 minutes.

- Turn bread over, place cheese rounds on bread, top with a tomato half. Broil until cheese is melted.

Submitted by Connie Laude
Serves 6   **Serv/Size** 2 pieces   **Cal/Serv** 250
Sodium 615mg   **Calcium** 260mg   **Cholesterol** 20mg
Fiber 3g   **Fat/Serv** 10g   **Fat** 38%

Exchanges: 1P,   1B

Sensibly Thin Shake

1/2 cup light vanilla ice cream
1/2 cup skim milk (calcium fortified)
1/2 cup fruit of your choice

- Blend slightly. **Do not** over-blend or shake will be runny!

Submitted by Sam
Serves 1   Serv/Size 1 1/2 cups   **Cal/Serv** 200
Sodium 118mg   **Calcium** 330mg   **Cholesterol** 7mg
Fiber 3g   **Fat/Serv** 2g   **Fat** 8%

Exchanges: 1B, 1M, 1Fr

Sam's Note:
Some of my favorite fruits to use in the Sensibly Thin Shake are; 1 cup strawberries, half a banana, 3/4 cup blueberries, or a peach. Frozen fruit makes a thicker shake.

Shower Punch

3 cups unsweetened pineapple juice
3 cups unsweetened pink grapefruit juice
1 quart Diet Squirt
1 1/2 quart low-fat frozen yogurt (any fruit flavor)

- Mix first three ingredients in punch bowl.

- In each glass, drop in 1/2 cup of fruit-flavored frozen yogurt.

- Add punch to glass.

- Serve immediately.

Submitted by Kathy Halvorson
Serves 12   **Serv/Size** 3/4 cup   **Cal/Serv** 155
Sodium 61mg   **Calcium** 90mg   **Cholesterol** 5mg
Fiber 0g   **Fat/Serv** 2g   **Fat** 9%

Exchanges: 1B, 1Fr

Cranberry Punch

1 bottle (64 oz.) low-calorie cranberry juice
1 bottle (2 liter) Fresca or Diet Squirt

- Mix 3/4 cup each, juice and soda. Garnish with a slice of lemon or orange (optional).

Submitted by Sam
Serves 1 Serv/Size 12 oz. Cal/Serv 35 Sodium 30mg
Cholesterol 0mg Fiber 0g Fat/Serv 0g Fat 0%
Exchanges: 1 serving FREE!
          2 servings = 1Fr

> *Sam's Note:*
> *This punch is pretty served in a wine glass, goblet or punch bowl.*

Delicious Non-Alcoholic Beverage

1 can (12 oz.) frozen Dole Pineapple-Banana-Orange Juice
Diet Squirt
- Mix juice concentrate per directions on can.
- Mix 3/4 cup juice, 3/4 cup Diet Squirt in a glass.

Submitted by Mary Ann Armbrust
Serves 1 Serv/Size 12 oz. Cal/Serv 95 Sodium 28mg
Cholesterol 0mg Fiber 0g Fat/Serv 0g Fat 1.5%
Exchanges: 1Fr

> *Sam's Note:*
> *I like to mix this beverage in a large glass pitcher and float strawberries, orange slices, and pineapple chunks. It makes an attractive presentation.*

Fantastically Fresh Lemonade

- Mix your favorite choice of unsweetened powdered summer beverage.

  If you choose:
- Lemonade, add fresh lemon slices.
- Citrus flavor, add lemon and orange slices.
- Fruit punch, add lemon, lime, orange slices, and strawberry halves.

Submitted by Sam (That clever gal!)
Serves 1   Serv/Size 12 oz.   **Cal/Serv** 5   **Sodium** 0mg
Cholesterol 0mg   **Fiber** 0g   **Fat/Serv** 0g   **Fat**

Exchanges: FREE!

Sunshine Tea

- Place 9 bags of regular or flavored tea in a gallon jar of water.
- Place in sunshine for 4 hours.

Exchanges: FREE!

Sam's Note:
Another brilliant idea! **Herbal** *tea can be counted as part of your daily water requirement because it does not contain caffeine. Caffeine is a natural diuretic which defeats the purpose of drinking eight glasses of water a day.*

Strawberry Banana Cooler

1 cup skim milk (calcium fortified)
1/2 banana
6 fresh strawberries
1 pkt. Equal

- In blender, mix all ingredients until smooth.

- Frozen fruit will make this thicker.

Submitted by Jeanne Waalen
Serves 1   Serv/Size 1 1/2 cup   Cal/Serv 170
Sodium 0mg   Calcium 500mg   Cholesterol 5mg
Fiber 4g   Fat/Serv 0g   Fat 4%

Exchanges: 1M, 1Fr

Sam's Note:
This is very thick and very refreshing, a great way to get a milk exchange for people who do not enjoy drinking milk! Amen!

Chicken Stew

2 boneless, skinless chicken breasts, cut in chunks
1 cup onion, diced
1 cup celery, chopped
1 cup green pepper, diced
1 can (32 oz.) tomatoes, with juice
1/2 cup frozen green beans
1/2 cup carrots, sliced
2 bay leaves
1 tsp. parsley
1 tsp. salt
1/2 tsp. thyme
1 tsp. basil
1/2 tsp. chili powder, to taste
1/8 tsp. pepper

- Combine all ingredients, cook over medium heat until chicken and vegetables are done. Remove bay leaves before serving.

- Better yet, try using the crock pot! Cook on low 4 to 6 hours.

Submitted by Kim Peterson
Serves 8   Serv/Size 1 1/4 cups   **Cal/Serv** 115
Sodium 750mg   **Cholesterol** 16mg   **Fiber** 3g
Fat/Serv 0g   **Fat** 5%

Exchanges: 1P, 2V

Easy Turkey Minestrone

12 oz. cooked turkey, cut up
2 cans (14.5 oz.) low-sodium chicken broth
1 can (16 oz.) stewed tomatoes
1 can (15 oz.) kidney beans, drained
1 cup frozen mixed vegetables
1/2 tsp. oregano
1 bay leaf
1 tsp. garlic powder
2 tsp. salt
fresh ground pepper to taste

- Combine ingredients.

- Bring to boil; reduce heat and simmer 1 hour. Before serving remove bay leaf.

Submitted by Jodi Hovell
Serves 6   **Serv/Size** 1 3/4 cups   **Cal/Serv** 190
Sodium 1200mg   **Cholesterol** 35mg   **Fiber** 19g
Fat/Serv 0g   **Fat** 4%

Exchanges: 3P,   1V

Sam's Note:
I like to use the turkey carcass. Throw in pot, cover with water, cook on low all day. To remove as much fat as possible, let the soup cool in refrigerator and skim off fat.

Cheesy Turkey Chowder (Fabulous)

1 cup onion, chopped
1 cup celery, chopped
2 cups carrots, grated
2 Tbsp. cornstarch
1 can (15 oz.) low-sodium chicken broth
2 cups skim milk (calcium fortified)
3/4 cup (3 oz.) light Cheddar cheese, shredded
6 oz. chicken or turkey, cooked and diced

- Sauté onions, celery, and carrots 2 minutes on high in microwave. Mix in cornstarch.
- In saucepan combine vegetables, broth, and milk. Stir on medium heat until mixture thickens.
- Add cheese and meat, continue to cook until the cheese melts. **Do not boil or cheese will separate.**

Submitted by Sam
Serves 4   **Serv/Size** 2 cups   **Cal/Serv** 235
Sodium 1100mg   **Calcium** 597mg   **Cholesterol** 71mg
Fiber 1.5g   **Fat/Serv** 4g   **Fat** 15%

Exchanges: 3P,   1/2B,   1V

Sam's Note:
*This is **the** recipe that sparked my interest in learning how to reduce fat, sodium and cholesterol so we could enjoy all our old favorite recipes. You would **never** believe what the original recipe was like. See the following page to find out.*

Cheesy Turkey Chowder
Original vs. Low-Calorie Comparison

Original

Ingredients	Calories
1 cup onions, chopped	100
1 cup celery, chopped	0
2 cup carrots, grated	0
1/4 cup butter	360
2 cups turkey or chicken broth	35
12 oz. sharp Cheddar, shredded	1,320
12 oz. cooked turkey or chicken, diced	650
1/4 cup flour	100
2 cups half and half	640
TOTAL	3,205

Serves	Cal/Serv	Sodium	Calcium
4	801	1490mg	785mg

Chol.	Fiber	Fat/Serv	Fat
71mg	2g	59g	66%

Low-Calorie

Ingredients	Calories
1 cup onions, chopped	100
1 cup celery, chopped	0
2 cups carrots, grated	0
none	0
2 cups turkey or chicken broth	35
6 oz. light sharp Cheddar, shredded	480
6 oz. cooked turkey or chicken, diced	325
2 Tbsp. cornstarch	100
2 cups skim milk (calcium fortified)	180
TOTAL	1,180

Serves	Cal/Serv	Sodium	Calcium
4	295	1100mg	597mg

Chol.	Fiber	Fat/Serv	Fat
215mg	1.5g	4g	15%

Vegetable Cheese Soup

1 pkg. (10 oz.) frozen mixed vegetables
1 small onion, diced
2 Tbsp. flour
1 tsp. Italian herb seasoning
1/8 tsp. pepper
1 tsp. chicken bouillon granules
1 cup water
1 cup skim milk (calcium fortified)
1 cup (4 oz.) light American or Cheddar cheese, shredded
2 tsp. Dijon mustard

- Rinse excess ice from mixed vegetables, combine with onion in saucepan.
- Mix flour, Italian seasoning, and pepper; coat vegetables.
- Dissolve bouillon granules in water and milk, add to saucepan. Bring to boil over medium heat, stirring constantly until thick and bubbly.
- Reduce heat to low, add cheese and mustard.
- **Do not boil**, or the cheese will separate. Stir to blend and serve immediately.

Submitted by Eileen Kaehler
Serves 6 **Serv/Size** 1 cup **Cal/Serv** 150
Sodium 760mg **Calcium** 360mg **Cholesterol** 11mg
Fiber 5g **Fat/Serv** 3g **Fat** 15%

Exchanges: 1P,   2V

Vegetarian Vegetable Soup

1/4 cup onion, chopped
2 carrots, chopped
2 celery stalks, chopped
2 cups frozen mixed vegetables
1 can (4 oz.) mushrooms, sliced
1 can (32 oz.) stewed tomatoes
1/4 cabbage head, chopped
2 cans (14.5 oz.) vegetable broth

- Sauté onions, carrots, and celery 2 minutes on high in microwave.

- Combine all ingredients together, bring to boil, simmer 20 minutes.

Serves 8   **Serv/Size** 1 1/4 cup   **Cal/Serv** 90
Sodium 1260mg   **Cholesterol** 0mg   **Fiber** 2g
Fat/Serv 1.5g   **Fat** 12%

Exchanges: 2V

Sam's Note:
Variations: Italian seasoning, garlic powder and 1 cup diced chicken may be added for Chicken Vegetable Soup. Chili powder, garlic powder and 1 cup beef may be added for Beef Vegetable Soup.

Cream of Broccoli Soup

1 bunch broccoli, cut in bite size pieces
2 chicken bouillon cubes
2 1/2 cups water
2 cups skim milk (calcium fortified)
3 Tbsp. cornstarch
2 tsp. margarine
1/2 tsp. white pepper
1 tsp. salt
1/4 tsp. curry
1/4 tsp. cumin

- Add broccoli and bouillon cubes to 2 1/2 cups boiling water, allow to boil 5 minutes.
- **Meanwhile, back at the ranch.** Combine milk, cornstarch, and margarine in saucepan. Cook over medium heat until thick, stir continuously.
- Add thickened sauce to broccoli and water mixture.
- Stir in seasonings, heat before serving.

Submitted by LuAnn Gross
Serves 4   **Serv/Size** 2 cups   **Cal/Serv** 105
Sodium 900mg   **Calcium** 290mg   **Cholesterol** 2mg
Fiber 1g   **Fat/Serv** 2g   **Fat** 15%

Exchanges: 1M, 1V

Sam's Note:
I love this soup. Curry and cumin add a wonderful flavor. If you do not care for curry, omit it. If you do not care for hot seasoned food, omit cumin

Corn Chowder

1 onion, chopped
2 medium potatoes, peeled and diced
4 cups hot skim milk (calcium fortified)
1/2 jar (2 oz.) real bacon pieces
1 can (16 oz.) creamed style corn

- Sauté onion 2 minutes on high in microwave.

- In saucepan cover potatoes with water; bring to boil. Cook until potatoes are tender, drain.

- Add milk to saucepan, simmer. Reduce heat.

- Just before serving, add onion, bacon, and corn. Heat thoroughly. **Do Not Boil.**

Submitted by Connie Laude
Serves 6   **Serv/Size** 2 cups   **Cal/Serv** 170
Sodium 314mg   **Calcium** 350mg   **Cholesterol** 7mg
Fiber 3g   **Fat/Serv** 2g   **Fat** 10%

Exchanges: 1 1/2B,   1M

Quick Beef Soup

1 lb. lean ground beef (no more than 10% fat)
2 cups carrots, sliced
1/4 cup onion, chopped
1 can (16 oz.) tomato sauce
1 can (4 oz.) mushrooms, sliced
2 cups water
2 tsp. salt
2 tsp. Worcestershire sauce
1/4 tsp. chili powder

- Brown ground beef in microwave, drain.

- Sauté carrots and onions 2 minutes on high in microwave.

- Combine all ingredients. Cover and simmer for 30 minutes, stir occasionally.

Submitted by Eileen Kaehler
Serves 8   Serv/Size 1 cup   **Cal/Serv** 90
Sodium 170mg   **Cholesterol** 20mg   **Fiber** trace
Fat/Serv 5g   **Fat** 51%

Exchanges: 1P,   1V

Chili Con Carne

1 lb. lean ground beef (no more than 10% fat)
2 medium onions, chopped
1/2 stalk celery, chopped
1 can (15 oz.) kidney beans, drained
1 can (14.5 oz.) tomatoes
1 tsp. salt
1/2 tsp. chili powder
4 cups water

- Brown lean ground beef, drain well.

- Add all other ingredients, simmer for 30 minutes.

Submitted by Sam
Serves 6   Serv/Size 2 cups   Cal/Serv 195
Sodium 1200mg   Cholesterol 27mg   Fiber 9g
Fat/Serv 7g   Fat 34%

Exchanges: 4P,   1B,   1V

Sam's Note:
How about a chili dog with the leftover chili? Use a light hot dog (45 cal.), 1/4 cup chili, and a light hot dog bun. 1 serving = 150 calories, 2 protein, 1 bread.

Tami's Taco Soup

1 lb. lean ground beef (no more than 10% fat)
1 medium onion, chopped
1 can (15 oz.) corn, drained
1 can (15 oz.) kidney beans, drained
1 can (32 oz.) tomato juice
1 pkg. taco seasoning
water

- Brown ground beef with onion in microwave, drain.

- Combine everything except water. Bring to boil, reduce heat and simmer for 20 minutes.

- Add water to reach desired consistency.

Submitted by Tami Buchholz, R.D.
Serves 6   **Serv/Size** 1 1/2 cups   **Cal/Serv** 230
Sodium 840mg   **Cholesterol** 27mg   **Fiber** 10g
Fat/Serv 7g   **Fat** 27%

Exchanges: 2P, 1B, 1V

Sam's Meal Ideas:
Place 1 oz. broken tortilla chips in bowl, serve soup over chips. Add a fresh salad made with shredded lettuce, tomato pieces, and shredded light cheese. Use Salsa for the dressing. 10 chips=1 bread exchange.

Bouillabaisse-Sam's Favorite

1/2 cup onion, chopped
1 clove garlic, minced
1/2 cup celery, chopped
1 can (14.5 oz.) tomatoes, peeled and diced
1 can (8 oz.) tomato sauce
3 tsp. paprika
2 cups water
1 tsp. basil
1/2 cup dry sherry or chicken bouillon
1 lb. shrimp
1 lb. Cod, cut in chunks
12 mock crab sticks **or** 12 oz. crab, cut in chunks

- Combine all ingredients, except Cod, in Crockpot.

- Cook on high 2 hours.

- Add Cod.

- Cover, cook 1 hour on high.

Serves 6   **Serv/Size** 1 1/2 cups   **Cal/Serv** 125
Sodium 650mg   **Calcium** 140mg   **Cholesterol** 190mg
Fiber 1g   **Fat/Serv** 3g   **Fat** 12%

Exchanges: 3P, 1V

Egg Drop Soup

2 cans (14.5 oz.) low-sodium chicken broth
1 Tbsp. cornstarch
2 eggs, beaten
2 Tbsp. green onions, sliced

- Combine cornstarch and chicken broth in saucepan. Stir until slightly thickened.

- Slowly pour eggs into broth, gently stir once using a fork.

- Remove from heat; pour into bowls, garnish with green onions.

Submitted by Sam
Serves 4　**Serv/Size** 1 cup　**Cal/Serv** 65　**Sodium** 515mg
Cholesterol 105mg　**Fiber** 0g　**Fat Serv** 2g　**Fat** 38%

Exchanges: 1/2P

Gaspacho Soup

2 hard cooked egg yokes, chopped
2 tsp. garlic powder
2 tsp. yellow mustard
2 tsp. Worcestershire sauce
1/2 tsp. chili powder
3 Tbsp. lemon juice
1 can (16 oz.) vegetable juice
1 jar (8 oz.) salsa
3 tomatoes, peeled and diced
1 onion, chopped
1 green pepper, chopped
1 cucumber, peeled, seeded and chopped
1 can (14.5 oz.) beef bouillon
1 avocado, peeled and diced

- Combine all ingredients. Chill overnight. Serve cold.

Submitted by Arlene Seminary
Serves 6   Serv/Size 1 1/4 cup   Cal/Serv 140
Sodium 560mg   Cholesterol 70mg   Fiber 3g
Fat/Serv 7g   Fat 40%

Exchanges: 2V, 2F

Sensibly Thin Pizza Sandwich

1/2 lb. lean ground beef (no more than 10% fat)
1 can (6 oz.) tomato paste
1/3 cup Parmesan cheese, grated
1/4 cup onion, finely chopped
1 can (2.25 oz.) pitted ripe olives, chopped
1/2 tsp. oregano
1 cup (4 oz.) Mozzarella cheese, shredded
8 tomato slices
4 English muffins

- Preheat oven to 300°.

- Brown ground beef, drain.

- Combine beef with next five ingredients.

- Toast English muffin halves. Top each half with a
  tomato slice, 2 Tbsp. meat, top with Mozzarella cheese.

- Bake 20 minutes or until cheese melts.

Submitted by Sam
Serves 4   Serv/Size both halves   **Cal/Serv** 398
Sodium 950mg   **Calcium** 380mg   **Cholesterol** 37mg
Fiber trace   **Fat/Serv** 15g   **Fat** 33%

Exchanges: 3P,   2B

Philly Beef Sandwich

1 green pepper, sliced
1 onion, sliced
1 slice (1 oz.) lean beef
1 slice (1 oz.) Mozzarella cheese
1 light bun

- Sauté green pepper and onion 2 minutes on high in microwave.

- **On bottom half of bun place:** beef, green pepper, onion and cheese.

- Broil until cheese melts, add top half bun.

Serves 1   **Cal/Serv** 203   **Sodium** 340 mg
Calcium 210mg   **Cholesterol** 30mg   **Fiber** 4.5g
Fat/Serv 7g   **Fat** 30%

Exchanges: 2P, 1B

Sam's Note:
If you use a regular bun, the exchange is 2 Breads.

Mini Sub

Choose:
1 light bun
1/2 pita (6" diameter) bread
Choose:
1 slice (1 oz.) ham, chicken, or roast beef
Choose:
1 slice (1 oz.) Mozzarella, Cheddar, or Monterey Jack
cheese
Choose any or all:
thin sliced tomatoes
shredded lettuce
sliced black olives (2 small)
thin sliced onion

- Make your own mini-sub by using a combination of the above, insert in a bun or 1/2 of a pita bread.
- Sprinkle with low-calorie Italian dressing. (6 cal. per Tbsp.) Serve light mayonnaise and mustard on the side.

Submitted by Sam
Serves 1   Cal/Serv 235   **Sodium** 330mg
Calcium 250mg   **Cholesterol** 40mg   **Fiber** 1g
Fat/Serv 10g   **Fat** 40%

Exchanges: 2P,   1B

Sam's Note:
This is a great lunch idea at the lake. Add fresh fruit and pickles. Teens especially love this when taking a 10 minute break from skiing. Company of all ages can make their own sandwich. It is a nice change from the standard lean ground beef on the grill.

Turkey Mini Pizza

2 oz. cooked turkey, chopped
1/4 cup pizza **or** spaghetti sauce
1 English muffin, split and toasted
2 slices (2 oz.) Mozzarella cheese

- Combine turkey and sauce, spoon on English muffin.

- Broil until turkey is heated.

- Top with cheese, broil until melted.

Submitted by Connie Laude
Serves 2 **Serv/Size** 1/2 muffin **Cal/Serv** 195
Sodium 330mg **Calcium** 255mg **Cholesterol** 40mg
Fiber trace **Fat/Serv** 8g **Fat** 28%

Exchanges: 2P, 1B, 1V

Turkey Melt

2 tomato slices
2 raw onion rings
2 green pepper rings
1 slice (1 oz.) turkey breast
1 Tbsp. low-calorie Italian dressing (6 cal. per Tbsp.)
1 slice (1 oz.) Monterey Jack cheese

- Place tomato slices, onion and green pepper rings on turkey breast.

- Sprinkle dressing on vegetables.

- Top with cheese.

- Broil until cheese melts.

Submitted by Sam
Serves 1   **Cal/Serv** 170   **Sodium** 285mg
Calcium 220mg   **Cholesterol** 43mg   **Fiber** 1g
Fat/Serv 9g   **Fat** 53%

Exchanges: 2P, 1V

Sam's Note:
I enjoy the Turkey Melt with a slice of light toast on the side. Some clients prefer a slice of toast under the Melt.
1 light bread = 40 calories and 1/2 bread exchange.

Hot Tuna Burgers

2 cans (6 oz.) water packed tuna, drained
1 cup celery, diced
1 cup (4 oz.) light Cheddar cheese, shredded
1/3 cup light mayonnaise
diced onion (optional)
4 light buns

- Preheat oven to 350°.

- Mix all ingredients. Measure 1/3 cup for each bun.

- Wrap each bun in foil and place on cookie sheet.

- Bake 20 minutes.

Submitted by Connie Laude
Serves 4   **Serv/Size** 1 bun   **Cal/Serv** 230   **Sodium** 890mg
Calcium 220mg   **Cholesterol** 48mg   **Fiber** trace
Fat/Serv 10g   **Fat** 39%

Exchanges: 2P, 1B, 2F

Sam's Note:
If you use regular buns, the exchange is 2 breads.
Instead of using foil to bake sandwiches, use brown
paper lunch bags, two buns per bag. This makes the
outside of the bun crisp, inside chewy.

Sensibly Thin Vegetable Salad

1 bunch broccoli
1 head cauliflower
1 cup celery, sliced
1 can (2.25 oz.) sliced ripe olives, drained
1 jar (4 oz.) sliced mushrooms, drained **or**
1 cup fresh, sliced
1 can (6 oz.) sliced water chestnuts, rinsed and drained
Mix:
1 bottle (8 oz.) low-cal. Italian dressing (6 cal. per Tbsp.)
1/4 tsp. pepper
2 tsp. dill
3 pkts. Equal

- Rinse first two vegetables, cut in bite size pieces.

- Combine vegetables and dressing early in the day, or day before. Stir or shake several times during the day to coat veggies.

- Salad will keep up to 3 days.

- Serve using slotted spoon.

Submitted by Sam
Serves 8   **Serv/Size** 1 cup   **Cal/Serv** 50   **Sodium** 350mg
Cholesterol 2mg   **Fiber** 2.5g   **Fat/Serv** 2g   **Fat** 25%

Exchanges: 1V

Sam's Note:
This veggie salad is rrrrreally high fiber.

Garden Fresh Salad

2 large tomatoes, sliced
1 medium onion, sliced
1 large green pepper, sliced
1 medium cucumber, sliced

Dressing:
3 Tbsp. vinegar
1/2 tsp. paprika
1/2 tsp. celery seed
2 Tbsp. oil
1/2 tsp. mustard

- Arrange vegetables in layers in 1 quart casserole.
- Mix together dressing ingredients.
- Pour over vegetables, refrigerate several hours.

Submitted by Sam
Serves 4   **Serv/Size** 3/4 cup   **Cal/Serv** 70   **Sodium** 15mg
Cholesterol 0mg   **Fiber** 2g   **Fat/Serv** 4g   **Fat** 45%

Exchanges: 1V, 1F

Sam's Note:
It takes 3,500 calories extra in your diet to gain one pound of body fat. I have never met anyone who gained a pound of body fat by eating too many vegetables.
1 cup raw or 1/2 cup cooked vegetables = 25 calories. You would need to eat 140 cups of raw veggies to equal 3,500 calories!!

Cauliflower Salad

1 head lettuce, torn in bite size pieces
1 small head cauliflower, cut in bite size pieces
1 red Bermuda onion, cut in rings
1/3 jar (2 oz.) real bacon pieces

Dressing:
3/4 cup light mayonnaise
2 Tbsp. skim milk (or to desired consistency)
2 pkts. Equal
1/3 cup Parmesan cheese, grated

- In bowl layer salad ingredients.

- Mix dressing, spread on salad.

- Refrigerate several hours to let flavors blend.

Serves 8   **Serv/Size** 1 1/2 cups   **Cal/Serv** 145
Sodium 320mg   **Calcium** 105mg   **Cholesterol** 12mg
Fiber 2.5g   **Fat/Serv** 9g   **Fat** 56%

Exchanges: 1V, 1 1/2F

Sam's Note:
If I know the whole salad will not be eaten, I mix the dressing and use only the amount needed. Salad does not keep once it has been tossed.

Broccoli Salad

1 head broccoli flowers, cut in bite size pieces
1 medium red onion, cut slices, then cut in half
2 Tbsp. sunflower seeds
1/3 jar (2 oz.) real bacon pieces
1/2 cup raisins
Mix together dressing:
1/4 cup light mayonnaise
1/4 cup light sour cream
skim milk (enough to thin dressing to ranch style
consistency)

- Combine vegetables and dressing, chill.

Submitted by Sam
Serves 6   **Serv/Size** 3/4 cup   **Cal/Serv** 140
Sodium 210mg   **Calcium** 50mg   **Cholesterol** 1mg
Fiber 2g   **Fat/Serv** 7g   **Fat** 40%

Exchanges: 2V, 1 1/2F

Sam's Note:
Do not use fat-free mayonnaise dressing for this salad.
Fat-Free does not contain oil, so the vegetables will
absorb the moisture, and the salad will become too
dry. Use light mayonnaise instead.

Sam's Summer Vegetable Salad

3 cups cooked (3 oz. dry wt.) macaroni **or** rainbow twirls

Add to pasta:
2 cups cauliflower, cut small
2 cups broccoli, cut small
4 or more green onions with stems, chopped
1/4 cup radishes, sliced (optional)

Dressing:
1/2 cup Parmesan cheese, grated
1/2 tsp. dill weed
1/2 tsp. garlic powder
1 bottle (8 oz.) low-cal. Italian dressing (6 cal. per Tbsp.)

• Add dressing mixture to salad.

Serves 6   **Serv/Size** 1 1/4 cup   **Cal/Serv** 175
Sodium 420mg   **Calcium** 140mg   **Cholesterol** 7mg
Fiber 2g   **Fat/Serv** 3g   **Fat** 15%

Exchanges: 1B,   2V

Sam's Note:
I love this salad!!!

Spaghetti Salad

1 large onion, chopped
1 green pepper, chopped
1 tomato, seeded and chopped
1 cucumber, peeled, seeded and chopped
Schilling Salad Supreme seasoning (no salt)
4 cups cooked (8 oz. dry wt.) spaghetti noodles **or**
rainbow twirls
1 bottle (8 oz.) light Italian dressing

- Combine vegetables.

- Pour 1/2 bottle Schilling Salad Supreme seasoning over vegetables, marinate overnight in refrigerator.

- Next day; cook pasta, mix with vegetables, toss with light dressing.

Submitted by Sam
Serves 8   Serv/Size 3/4 cup **Cal/Serv** 110
Sodium 220mg   **Cholesterol** 2mg   **Fiber** 2g
Fat/Serv 1g   **Fat** 6%

Exchanges: 1B,   1V

Sam's Note:
The original recipe used spaghetti noodles. I find it easier to eat using a smaller pasta. The spaghetti tended to splatter the dressing on my clothes, especially when I slurped the noodles between my lips.

Green Bean Salad

1 can (16 oz.) cut green beans, drained
2 cups frozen peas, rinsed
1/4 cup stuffed green olives, sliced
1/2 cup red onion, chopped
1 cup celery, chopped
Marinate the above ingredients overnight in the following:
2 Tbsp. oil
1/4 cup vinegar
1/4 tsp. garlic salt
1/2 tsp. paprika
1 pkt. Equal or 1 Tbsp. sugar
- When ready to serve, sprinkle top with 2 Tbsp. slivered toasted almonds.

Submitted by Sam
Serves 8   **Serv/Size** 3/4 cup   **Cal/Serv** 60   **Sodium** 360mg
Calcium 60mg   **Cholesterol** 0mg   **Fiber** 4g
Fat/Serv 3g   **Fat** 42%
Exchanges: 1V

Sam' Note:
If you know you are not going to eat all the green bean salad at one meal, do not use all the almonds. They tend to get soggy if left in the salad overnight. This salad keeps easily for five days, it's great with sandwiches the rest of the week.
I like to keep a jar of green stuffed salad olives. They are already sliced and I use just a few in my spaghetti, meat loaf, and other salads.
It is also easy to double this recipe. Bring it to potlucks. You will be asked for the recipe, be sure to tell them about the book! Thanks, **Sam**

Oriental Chicken Salad

Dressing:
5 Tbsp. white vinegar
1/4 cup oil
3 Tbsp. sugar
flavor packet from 1 pkg. chicken Ramen noodles
Salad:
8 oz. cooked chicken, cubed
1 lb. cabbage, shredded
3 green onions, chopped
2 pkgs. (3 oz.) low-fat Chicken Ramen noodles
4 Tbsp. sesame seeds, toasted
1/4 cup slivered almonds, toasted

- Combine dressing ingredients, cover. Refrigerate 4 hours or overnight.
- Break apart and broil Ramen noodles until light brown.
- Combine salad ingredients.
- Add dressing, toss. Serve with slotted spoon.

Submitted by Jacque Waalen
Serves 8   **Serv/Size** 3/4 cup   **Cal/Serv** 285
Sodium 125mg   **Calcium** 64mg   **Cholesterol** 16mg
Fiber 1.5g   **Fat/Serv** 5g   **Fat** 42%

Exchanges: 1P, 1B, 1V, 1F

Sam's Note:
To save time I toast a whole can of sesame seeds,
and place them back in the can for future recipes.
Remember sesame seeds, like all seeds have oil.
1 Tbsp. = 1 fat or 45 calories.

Ramen Noodle Salad

1 head cabbage, chopped
1 bunch green onions with tops, chopped
Marinate in:
1/4 cup oil
3 pkts. Equal
3 Tbsp. vinegar
1/2 tsp. pepper
Broil:
1 pkg. (3 oz.) low-fat Ramen noodles, crushed
2 Tbsp. sesame seeds
1 small pkg. slivered almonds
light soy sauce sprinkled on top

- Just before serving, toss together cabbage and noodle mixture. Serve with slotted spoon.

Submitted by Sam
Serves 8   Serv/Size 3/4 cup   **Cal/Serv** 110
Sodium 85mg   **Calcium** 60mg   **Cholesterol** 0mg
Fiber 1g   **Fat/Serv** 5g   **Fat** 42%

Exchanges: 1/2B, 1V, 1F

Sam's Note:
If you are not going to eat all the salad, save some noodle mixture to use later. If you were using the exchange program you would see there could actually be 2 fats per serving. This really is not true because you are using a slotted spoon to drain some of the dressing off, and you will not pick up your plate and licked it clean.

Patio Slaw

1 head cabbage, shredded
1/2 green pepper, chopped
1/2 red pepper, chopped
1/2 red onion, chopped
3 celery stalks, chopped

Dressing:
3/4 cup white vinegar
1/4 cup water
2 Tbsp. sugar **or** 2 pkts. Equal
1 tsp. celery seeds
1 tsp. mustard seeds

- Pour 1 1/2 cups cold water over first four ingredients, let stand in the refrigerator several hours.
- In saucepan, combine dressing, bring to a boil. Cool in refrigerator.
- Drain water from salad, add celery.
- Combine dressing and salad.

Serves 8   **Serv/Size** 3/4 cup   **Cal/Serv** 45   **Sodium** 40mg
Calcium 95mg   **Cholesterol** 0mg   **Fiber** 2g
Fat/Serv 0g   **Fat** 9%
Exchanges: 1V (with Equal)
             1Fr,   1V (with sugar)

Sam's Note:
*Because of the amount of carbohydrates, 22 grams are sugar. This equals one Fruit Exchange. However, using sugar for a fruit exchange cheats us of vitamins A &C. If you prefer using 3 pkts. Equal there is not a fruit exchange. The reason for using sugar in a recipe is to make the dressing a little thicker. Although, this is **my** recipe, maybe you should **just leave it alone**.*

Turkey Summer Salad

12 oz. cooked turkey, diced
1 cup celery, diced
1 can (11 oz.) mandarin oranges, drained
30 grapes, halved
1 can (8 oz.) chunked pineapple in own juice, drained and reserve juice
Mix together dressing:
1/2 cup light mayonnaise
juice from pineapple
2 tsp. vinegar
1 pkt. Equal

- Toss salad ingredients together with dressing.

- **Optional:** 2 cups cooked macaroni which would add
  1 bread per person, 80 calories more per serving.

Serves 4 **Serv/Size** 1 1/2 cups **Cal/Serv** 285
Sodium 300mg **Calcium** 105mg **Cholesterol** 60mg
Fiber 1.5g **Fat/Serv** 9g **Fat** 34%

Exchanges: 3P, 2Fr, 2F

Caesar Salad

2 heads romaine lettuce
3 to 4 garlic cloves
1/2 cup olive oil
1/2 tsp. salt
1/2 tsp. pepper
1 tsp. Worcestershire sauce
1/4 cup lemon juice
1 egg, boiled and chopped
1/4 cup fresh Parmesan, grated
5 anchovies, chopped (optional)

- Wash lettuce, tear in bite size pieces.

- Marinate garlic in olive oil for a minimum of 30 minutes. The longer the better.

- Strain oil to remove garlic. Mix oil with next four ingredients. The longer this dressing stands, the better it will taste. Dressing lasts weeks in the refrigerator.

- Pour 1/2 cup dressing over romaine, toss with remaining ingredients. If you don't like anchovies, just rub the bowl with them for flavor.

Submitted by Sam
Serves 8   Serv/Size divide evenly   **Cal/Serv** 95
Sodium 150mg   **Calcium** 65mg   **Cholesterol** 30mg
Fiber 0g   **Fat/Serv** 7g   **Fat** 75%

Exchanges: 1V,   1 1/2F

Wilted Lettuce Salad

1 head Romaine lettuce
4 bacon slices, crumbled
1 bunch green onions, sliced
1/4 cup sugar
salt and pepper to taste
1/2 cup vinegar
1/4 cup water

- Wash lettuce, tear in bite size pieces. Combine with bacon and green onions.

- In saucepan combine rest of ingredients. Simmer until hot.

- Pour dressing over lettuce.

Submitted by Jean Bassett
Serves 4 **Serv/Size** 1/4 **Cal/Serv** 100 **Sodium** 470mg
Calcium 70mg **Cholesterol** 10mg **Fiber** trace
Fat/Serv 4g **Fat** 27%

Exchanges: 1/2Fr, 1F

Spinach Salad

1 bunch spinach, rinsed and dried
1/2 jar (2 oz.) real bacon pieces
1/4 cup green onions, chopped
2 eggs, boiled and chopped
1 cup croutons
Dressing:
1 Tbsp. sugar
3/4 tsp. salt
1/2 tsp. dry mustard
3/4 tsp. paprika
1/8 tsp. pepper
1/4 cup oil
3 Tbsp. white vinegar
1 Tbsp. extra dry vermouth (optional)

- Combine dressing ingredients, shake well. Allow to stand at least 1 hour.

- Combine salad ingredients, except croutons.

- Right before serving, toss salad with dressing and croutons.

Submitted by Betty Witham
Serves 4   **Serv/Size** 1/4   **Cal/Serv** 165   **Sodium** 580mg
Calcium 148mg   **Cholesterol** 110mg   **Fiber** 3g
Fat/Serv 12g   **Fat** 60%

Exchanges: 1/2B, 1V, 2F

Spring Time Salad

2 bunches fresh spinach, rinsed and drained
1 pint strawberries, halved
Mix dressing in blender:
1/3 cup sugar
2 Tbsp. sesame seeds, toasted
1 Tbsp. poppy seeds
1 1/2 tsp. onion, minced
1/4 tsp. Worcestershire sauce
1/4 tsp. paprika
1/3 cup oil
3 Tbsp. cider vinegar

- Place spinach on salad plate, top with strawberries.

- Drizzle dressing over salad.

Submitted by Eileen Kaehler
Serves 8   Serv/Size 2 Tbsp. dressing   **Cal/Serv** 120
Sodium 65mg   **Calcium** 145mg   **Cholesterol** 0mg
Fiber 4g (WHOA!)   **Fat/Serv** 9g   **Fat** 57%

Exchanges: 1/2Fr, 1V, 1F

> *Sam's Note:*
> *I hate cleaning spinach, so I buy it in the bag and skip the sand.*

Sensibly Thin Romaine Salad

1 bunch Romaine lettuce, torn into bite size pieces
1/2 jar (2oz.) real bacon pieces
2 Tbsp. sesame seeds, toasted
Dressing:
1/2 cup oil
1/2 cup red wine vinegar
3 pkts. Equal
1 tsp. salt
2 tsp. garlic powder

- Mix dressing, refrigerate.

- Combine lettuce, bacon pieces, and sesame seeds.

- Toss lettuce with half the dressing.

- Serve immediately.

Submitted by Sam
Serves 4 **Serv/Size** 1/4 **Cal/Serv** 75 **Sodium** 170mg
Calcium 310mg **Cholesterol** 5mg **Fiber** 0g
Fat/Serv 7g **Fat** 40%

Exchanges: 1V, 1F

Sam's Note:
If you enjoy the dressing and want to use it on a salad later, 2 Tbsp. = 1 Fat.

Cranberry Celery Salad

1 pkg. (.3 oz.) sugar-free cranberry Jello
1 cup boiling water
1/2 cup cold water
1 Tbsp. lemon juice
1 pkg. (12 oz.) coarsely ground cranberries
1 cup celery, chopped
orange rind (optional)
(What else did your Grandma put in it?)

- Prepare Jello as directed. Chill until partially set.

- Add rest of ingredients.

- Pour into an 8x8" dish or 4 cup mold. Chill and set.

- Serve on lettuce.

Submitted by Sam
Serves 6   **Serv/Size** 1/6 or 2/3 cup   **Cal/Serv** 20
Sodium 30mg   **Cholesterol** 0mg   **Fiber** 1.5g
Fat/Serv trace   **Fat** 2%

Exchanges: FREE!
              3 servings=1Fr

Sam's Note:
*I love cranberries. Most people do not realize how high in calories **canned** cranberries are, 2 Tbsp. = 60 calories. Can you believe it? What a bummer. What a great substitute this recipe is.*

Raw Cranberry Salad

1 pkg. (12 oz.) raw cranberries, ground
1 cup sugar
1 1/2 cups Light Cool Whip
1 can (8 oz.) crushed pineapple, drained
2 cups mini marshmallows

- Sprinkle sugar over cranberries, let set 2 hours.

- Mix with remaining ingredients, refrigerate overnight in a 9x13" dish.

- Freezes well.

Submitted by Kathy Halvorson
Serves 12   **Serv/Size** 1/12 or 1/2 cup   **Cal/Serv** 175
Sodium trace   **Cholesterol** 0mg   **Fiber** 2g
Fat/Serv 2g   **Fat** 12%

Exchanges: 2Fr

Cherry Jello Salad

1 1/2 cups boiling **diet** water (ba ha ha)
1 can (16 oz.) light cherry pie filling
2 pkgs. (.3 oz.) sugar-free cherry Jello
1/2 can (12 oz.) diet cola

- In saucepan mix together first three ingredients, simmer 5 minutes.

- Stir in diet cola.

- Chill until set.

- Feel free to drink the remaining diet cola.

Submitted by Dorene Tollefson
Serves 6   **Serv/Size** 3/4 cup   **Cal/Serv** 60   **Sodium** 30mg
Cholesterol 0mg   **Fiber** 1g   **Fat/Serv** 0g   **Fat** 0%

Exchanges: 1Fr

Sam's Note:
My favorite diet cola is diet Pepsi. ***(what's your opinion Ann?)***

Pineapple Lime Salad

1 container (12 oz.) non-fat cottage cheese
1 pkg. (.3 oz.) sugar-free lime Jello (or other favorite)
1 can (20 oz.) crushed pineapple, drained
1/2 cup Light Cool Whip

- Sprinkle Jello over cottage cheese. Mix well.

- Add other ingredients.

- May be made with or without Cool Whip.

Submitted by Linda Finneman
Serves 6 **Serv/Size** 3/4 cup **Cal/Serv** 110
Sodium 237mg **Cholesterol** 2mg **Fiber** trace
Fat/Serv 1g **Fat** 10%

Exchanges: 1/2P, 1Fr

Sam's Fruit Salad

1 can (20 oz.) pineapple chunks, **do not drain**
1 can (15 oz.) chunky fruit cocktail, **drained**
1 pkg. (1 oz.) sugar-free instant vanilla **or** banana pudding
1/2 cup Cool Whip

- Mix together first three ingredients.

- Fold in Cool Whip.

Submitted by The Head Banana
Serves 8   **Serv/Size** 1/2 cup   **Cal/Serv** 85
Sodium 170mg   **Cholesterol** 0mg   **Fiber** 1g
Fat/Serv 0g   **Fat** 5%

Exchanges: 1Fr

Sam's Note:
*I chose regular Cool Whip for this recipe. I have
found in certain recipes that Light Cool Whip
separates if it sits overnight. There is a 60 calorie
difference between regular and Light Cool Whip. That
make this entire recipe only 30 calories higher.*

Ambrosia Fruit Salad

1 container (8 oz.) light sour cream (do not use fat-free)
1 cup mini marshmallows
1/4 cup coconut
1 can (14 oz.) pineapple chunks, drained
1 can (11 oz.) mandarin oranges, drained

- Mix ingredients together. Chill before serving.

Submitted by LeAnn Zogg
Serves 8   Serv/Size 3/4 cup   **Cal/Serv** 110
Sodium 60mg   **Cholesterol** 10mg   **Fiber** trace
Fat/Serv 3g   **Fat** 24%

Exchanges: 1Fr, 1/2F

Frozen Fruit Cups

1 can (6 oz.) frozen orange juice concentrate
3 Tbsp. lemon juice
1 can (11 oz.) mandarin oranges, drained
1 bag (10 oz.) sugar-free frozen strawberries
1 can (20 oz.) crushed pineapple, in own juice
3 sliced bananas

- Cut strawberries in half.

- Mix all ingredients together.

- Divide evenly into a dozen paper lined muffin pan, freeze.

- Take out of freezer 20 minutes before serving.

Submitted by Shirley Disher
Serves 12   **Serv/Size** 3/4 cup   **Cal/Serv** 60   **Sodium** 2mg
Cholesterol 0mg   **Fiber** 1.5g   **Fat/Serv** trace   **Fat** 4%

Exchanges: 1Fr

Curried Fruit

1 can (16 oz.) pear halves, **drained**
6 maraschino cherries
1 can (16 oz.) cling peaches or apricots, **drained**
1 can (20 oz.) pineapple slices, **reserve juice**
1/4 cup brown sugar
1 tsp. curry powder

- Preheat oven to 325°.

- Place fruit in 2 quart baking dish.

- Combine brown sugar and curry, add to fruit, stir gently.

- Bake 30 minutes. Baste once during cooking.

- **Delicious served with wild game, or ham.**

Submitted by Barb Holter
Serves 12   Serv/Size 3/4 cup   **Cal/Serv** 90
Sodium 8mg   **Cholesterol** 0mg   **Fiber** 1.5g
Fat/Serv 0g   **Fat** 0%

Exchanges: 1Fr

Potato Salad

2 lbs. potatoes, peeled, cut in 1" cubes
1 cup celery, chopped
1 cup green bell pepper, chopped
1/2 cup onion, finely chopped
1/2 cup dill pickles, finely chopped
Dressing:
1/2 cup light mayonnaise
1/2 cup plain non-fat yogurt
1/4 cup dill pickle juice
1 Tbsp. Dijon mustard
1 tsp. salt
1/2 tsp. pepper

- Cook potatoes in boiling water until tender. Drain and cool.
- Whisk dressing until blended.
- Combine potatoes and remaining ingredients. Toss gently with dressing to coat.
- Chill.

Submitted by Carla Hansen
Serves 8 Serv/Size 1 cup Cal/Serv 180
Sodium 500mg Cholesterol 0mg Fiber 4g
Fat/Serv 4g Fat 17%

Exchanges: 2B, 1F

Sam's Note:
Do not use fat-free mayonnaise. The potatoes absorb the liquid and the potato salad will be dry.

Warm German Potato Salad

2 lbs. potatoes, cut in 1/4" slices
1/2 cup onion, chopped
1 jar (2 oz.) chopped pimento, drained
1 jar (2 oz.) real bacon pieces
Dressing:
1 cup low-sodium beef broth
3/4 cup cider vinegar
2 Tbsp. oil
2 Tbsp. flour
2 Tbsp. sugar
1/2 tsp. salt
1/2 tsp. celery seed
1/4 tsp. pepper

- Cook potatoes until tender, drain.
- Add onion, pimento, and bacon.
- Place dressing ingredients in skillet. Blend.
- Bring to a boil, whisking often. Reduce heat, simmer 2-3 minutes until thickened.
- Pour dressing over potato mixture, toss gently to coat.
- Serve warm.

Submitted by Carla Hansen
Serves 8 **Serv/Size** 3/4 cup **Cal/Serv** 175
Sodium 320mg **Cholesterol** 5mg **Fiber** 2.6g
Fat/Serv 5g **Fat** 27%

Exchanges: 2B, 1F

Sam's Note:
I like this recipe with grilled pork chops.

Chow Mein

2 to 3 cups cabbage, chopped
2 to 3 cups celery, chopped
2 1/2 cups water
3 chicken bouillon cubes
1 large onion, chopped
1 can (14 oz.) bean sprouts, rinsed and drained
1 can (4 oz.) mushrooms, drained
12 oz. cooked chicken or turkey, chopped
2 cups cooked rice

- Combine and simmer together first five ingredients until tender crisp.

- Add remaining ingredients, except rice.

- Simmer for 15 minutes.

- Serve over 1/2 cup rice.

Submitted by Julie Williams
Serves 4   **Serv/Size** 2 cups over 1/2 cup rice
Cal/Serv 220   **Sodium** 1014mg   **Calcium** 80mg
Cholesterol 50mg   **Fiber** 2.5g   **Fat/Serv** 3g   **Fat** 12%

Exchanges: 3P, 1B, 1V

Sam's Note:
This is a great way to use up leftover turkey!

Chop Suey

6 oz. cooked beef, chicken, or shrimp
1 can (4 oz.) tomatoes
1 Tbsp. onion flakes
4 celery stocks, cut in chunks
1/2 cup green pepper, chopped
2 cups bean sprouts, use generously
light soy sauce

- Slice meat thin or leave shrimp whole.

- Add next four ingredients.

- Rinse sprouts and add last.

- Simmer 10 minutes.

- Flavor with soy sauce.

Submitted by Sam
Serves 2   **Serv/Size** 1 1/2 cups   **Cal/Serv** 160
Sodium 255mg   **Calcium** 69mg   **Cholesterol** 50mg
Fiber 5g   **Fat/Serv** 2g   **Fat** 12%

Exchanges: 3P, 2V

Sam's Note:
Soy Sauce has very few calories (1 Tbsp. = 10 calories).
However, the sodium is outrageous (1 Tbsp. = 605mg).
Low sodium is only 75mg for the same amount.

Oriental Chicken

1/4 cup light soy sauce
2 Tbsp. cornstarch
1 tsp. sugar
4 boneless, skinless chicken breasts, cut in 1" pieces
1/2 lb. pea pods
1/2 lb. fresh mushrooms
1 can (6 oz.) bamboo shoots, sliced in 1/4" pieces
1 Tbsp. oil
1 cup chicken broth
1/2 cup cashews (optional)

- Combine soy sauce, cornstarch, and sugar. Add chicken, marinate about 15 minutes.
- Wash pea pods, remove ends and strings. Brush mushrooms, rinse and drain bamboo shoots, set aside.
- Heat skillet with 1 Tbsp. oil. Using slotted spoon, remove chicken from marinade, set marinade aside. Cook chicken 2 minutes.
- Add peas, mushrooms, bamboo shoots, and broth.
- Cover and simmer 2 minutes, add marinade.
- Cook until thickened, stirring constantly.
- Sprinkle with cashews (1 Tbsp. = 1 fat).

Serves 4   **Serv/Size** 1 1/4 cup   **Cal/Serv** 215
Sodium 375mg   **Cholesterol** 49mg   **Fiber** 3g
Fat/Serv 6g   **Fat** 23%
Exchanges: 3P,   1V,   1F (without cashews)
          2 1/2F (with cashews) add 110 cal. per serv.

Sam's Note:
Do not wash mushrooms or they will become water soaked. Mushrooms act like a sponge in water. Brush mushrooms with a mushroom brush, or with a damp paper towel.

Curried Chicken

1 medium apple, peeled and chopped
1 small onion, chopped
1/4-1/2 tsp. curry powder
1 can (10.75 oz.) cream of mushroom soup
1 cup light sour cream
4 boneless, skinless chicken breasts

- Preheat oven to 350°.

- Sauté apple, onion, and curry in microwave for
  2 minutes on high.

- Mix soup and sour cream together. Blend with apple
  mixture. Pour over chicken.

- Bake covered for 25 minutes.

Submitted by Sam
Serves 4 **Serv/Size** 1 breast **Cal/Serv** 260
Sodium 750mg **Cholesterol** 50mg **Fiber** trace
Fat/Serv 7g **Fat** 25%

Exchanges: 3P, 1B, 1F

Oriental Curried Chicken

4 boneless, skinless chicken breasts, cut in thin strips
1 tsp. garlic powder
1/4 cup light soy sauce
1 cup beef bouillon
1 tsp. sugar
1 can (16 oz.) bean sprouts, rinsed and drained
1 can (4 oz.) mushrooms and juice
2 Tbsp. onion flakes
1/8 tsp. curry powder
pinch of ginger
2 stalks celery, chunked
1 green pepper, sliced
2 cups cooked rice

- Stir together chicken, garlic powder, and soy sauce, sauté in non-stick skillet on high for 3 minutes.

- Mix bouillon and sugar together, add next five ingredients.

- Pour over chicken, cover, cook for 3 minutes.

- Add celery and green pepper. Cook covered 2 minutes.

- Serve over 1/2 cup rice.

Submitted by Sam
Serves 4   **Serv/Size** 1 1/2 cups sauce   **Cal/Serv** 210
Sodium 913mg   **Cholesterol** 49mg   **Fiber** 2g
Fat/Serv 2g   **Fat** 10%

Exchanges: 3P, 1B, 1V

Chicken Oriental

Important! Prepare all ingredients before beginning.

Combine and set aside:
1/2 cup chicken broth
2 tsp. white wine or sherry (optional)
1/4 tsp. powdered ginger
1 tsp. light soy sauce
Combine and set aside:
1 tsp. cornstarch
1 Tbsp. cold water
dash pepper
Stir fry using 1/2 Tbsp. peanut, or vegetable oil:
1/2 cup onion, chopped, 1 minute (push onion to sides)
Stir fry 2 minutes using remaining oil:
4 boneless, skinless chicken breasts, thinly sliced
Add and stir fry 1 minute:
4 cups stir fry vegetables, (fresh or frozen)
Mix above ingredients together.
Add and heat for 1 minute uncovered:
chicken broth mixture
1 can (6 oz.) bamboo shoots, sliced, rinsed and drained
1 can (6 oz.) water chestnuts, sliced, rinsed and drained
Stir in cornstarch mixture, heat until thickened.
Serve over:
1/2 cup rice or chinese noodles.

Submitted by Dorothy Bjornson
Serves 4 **Serv/Size** 1 1/2 cups **Cal/Serv** 275 **Sodium**
800mg **Cholesterol** 50mg **Fiber** 3.5g **Fat/Serv** 5g **Fat**
15%
Exchanges: 3P, 1B, 2V, 1F

Mid-Eastern Style Chicken Breasts

4 boneless, skinless chicken breasts, pounded flat
1/3 cup onion, minced
1/2 cup chicken broth
1/4 cup currants or raisins
1/2 tsp. ground cumin
1/2 cup plain non-fat yogurt
1/2 cup fresh mint leaves or 2 Tbsp. dried mint

- Sauté chicken in non-stick skillet using 2 to 4 Tbsp. water. Cook 3-4 minutes each side. Remove to a plate.

- Add onion, broth, currants, and cumin. Boil about 2 minutes. Remove from heat; whisk in yogurt and mint. **Do not boil.**

- Return chicken to skillet. Turn to coat. Simmer 1-2 minutes. **Do not overcook or yogurt will separate.**

Submitted by Carla Hansen
Serves 4   **Serv/Size** 1 breast   **Cal/Serv** 160
Sodium 148mg   **Calcium** 115mg   **Cholesterol** 50mg
Fiber trace   **Fat/Serv** 2g   **Fat** 10%

Exchanges: 3P,   1/2Fr

Sam's Note:
Mix 1 Tbsp. cornstarch into yogurt to prevent separating, or strain yogurt.

Mediterranean Chicken

Important!! Prepare all ingredients before beginning.

1 can (8 oz.) pineapple chunks, drained, reserve juice

Sauté in skillet, (coated with non-stick spray):
4 boneless, skinless chicken breasts
1 small zucchini, cut in half lengthwise, sliced thin
1 carrot, sliced thin, diagonally
6 green onions, sliced thin, diagonally 1/2"

In saucepan combine following ingredients, stirring over low-heat until thickened:
pineapple juice
1 Tbsp. cornstarch
1/2 tsp. dry mustard
1/2 tsp. ground ginger
1/2 tsp. cilantro **or** 1 tsp. coriander
2 Tbsp. light soy sauce
2 Tbsp. ketchup or reduced-calorie Russian dressing
Add pineapple chunks to saucepan, heat.
Add sauce to skillet. Mix all ingredients together.

Submitted by Sam
Serves 4   Serv/Size 1 1/4 cup   Cal/Serv 190
Sodium 650mg   Calcium 55mg   Cholesterol 50mg
Fiber 2g   Fat/Serv 2g   Fat 10%

Exchanges: 3P, 1/2Fr, 1V

Sam's Serving Suggestion:
Serve over 1/2 cup cooked rice or couscous.

Chicken and Rice

4 boneless, skinless chicken breasts
1 cup rice
1 can (10.75 oz.) low-fat cream of mushroom soup
1/2 cup skim milk (calcium fortified)
1 pkg. dry onion soup mix
paprika

- Preheat oven to 350°.

- Place chicken in a casserole coated with non-stick spray.

- Combine next four ingredients, pour over chicken, sprinkle with paprika.

- Bake covered 1 hour.

Submitted by Connie Laude
Serves 4   **Serv/Size** 1 breast - 1/2 cup rice   **Cal/Serv** 245
Sodium 980mg   **Calcium** 150mg   **Cholesterol** 50mg
Fiber trace   **Fat/Serv** 4g   **Fat** 13%

Exchanges: 3P, 1B, 1F

Poppy Seed Chicken

4 boneless, skinless chicken breasts
12 Ritz crackers
1 Tbsp. margarine
2 Tbsp. poppy seeds
1 can (10.75 oz.) cream of chicken soup
1 carton (8 oz.) light sour cream

- Preheat oven to 350°.

- Cut chicken into chunks.

- Crush Ritz crackers, melt margarine. Mix together, add poppy seeds.

- Combine soup and sour cream.

- In a 2 1/2 quart casserole coated with non-stick spray layer 1/2 each: chicken, soup mixture, and crackers. Repeat.

- Bake uncovered for 30 minutes.

Submitted by Karen Swift
Serves 4   **Serv/Size** 1 cup   **Cal/Serv** 260   **Sodium** 826mg
Calcium 60mg   **Cholesterol** 60mg   **Fiber** 0g
Fat/Serv 11g   **Fat** 44%

Exchanges: 3P,   1B,   2F

Creamed Soup Substitute

2 cups non-fat dry milk
3/4 cup cornstarch
1/4 cup chicken bouillon granules
2 Tbsp. minced onion
1/4 tsp. pepper
1 tsp. dried thyme
1 tsp. basil

- Mix together all ingredients. Store in an airtight container. This will make the equivalent of 9 cans creamed soup.
- Use 1/3 cup mix and 1 1/4 cups water.
- Cook and stir until thick.

Submitted by Helen Punton
Cal/Serv 150   **Serv/Size** 1 1/4 cup equivalent to 1 can cream soup   **Sodium** 270mg   **Calcium** 350mg
Cholesterol 5mg   **Fiber** 0g   **Fat/Serv** 0g   **Fat** 2%

Sam's Note:
Substitute this recipe in place of 1 can cream soup.
Mushroom soup, add diced mushrooms.
Celery soup, add diced celery. (You get the drift.)
You will save 125 calories by using this recipe in place of a regular can of creamed soup.
The sodium content is the biggest difference.
2300mg of sodium in a can of regular cream soup,
1200mg of sodium in low-fat, less sodium soup.
WOW!

Chicken Casserole

1 bag (8 oz.) herb seasoned stuffing
12 oz. cooked chicken or turkey, diced
1/2 cup onion, chopped
1/2 cup celery, chopped
1/4 cup dehydrated chives **or** 2 Tbsp. fresh
1/2 cup light mayonnaise
3 egg whites
1 cup skim milk (calcium fortified)
1 can (10.75 oz.) low-fat cream of mushroom soup
1/4 cup (1 oz.) light Cheddar cheese, shredded

- Preheat oven to 325°.
- Place half bag of stuffing in bottom of a 9x13" baking dish coated with non-stick spray.
- Mix together next five ingredients, spread over stuffing. Top with remaining stuffing.
- Beat egg whites, milk, and soup together, blend. Pour over top of stuffing.
- Cover with foil, refrigerate overnight.
- Bake uncovered 40 minutes.
- Sprinkle with cheese, bake 5 minutes, or until cheese melts.

Submitted by Barb Holter
Serves 8   Serv/Size 1 cup   **Cal/Serv** 245   **Sodium** 660mg
Calcium 75mg   **Cholesterol** 35mg   **Fiber** 2g
Fat/Serv 9g   **Fat** 32%

Exchanges: 3P, 1B, 1F

Sam's Note:
This is a great recipe for pot lucks.

Easy Chicken and Broccoli

3/4 cup low-sodium chicken broth
2 Tbsp. oyster sauce
2 tsp. cornstarch
1 clove garlic, minced
1/2 tsp. fresh ginger root, minced or 1/4 tsp. ground ginger
2 boneless, skinless chicken breasts, cut in 1" strips
4 broccoli spears, cut in 1" pieces

- In small saucepan, combine first five ingredients. Cook over low heat, stirring occasionally until thickened.

- In skillet sauté chicken and broccoli in 2 Tbsp. water, 2 minutes, Cover, let simmer 5 minutes.

- Add broth mixture to chicken, stir together, heat.

Submitted by Beth Anderson
Serves 2   **Serv/Size** half recipe or 1 cup   **Cal/Serv** 140
Sodium 785mg   **Cholesterol** 50mg   **Fiber** trace
Fat/Serv 2g   **Fat** 10%

Exchanges: 3P,   1V

Stove-Top Chicken Broccoli

4 boneless, skinless chicken breasts, cut in chunks
1 head broccoli, cut in bite size pieces
1/4 cup onion, chopped
dash of garlic
1 tsp. lemon juice
1/4 tsp. Italian seasoning
3 medium tomatoes, wedged
2 cups cooked noodles

- Season chicken to taste using salt and pepper.

- Sauté next five ingredients in non-stick skillet, cover, simmer 5 minutes.

- Add tomatoes. Cover, simmer 2 minutes. Do not overcook.

- Serve over 1/2 cup noodles.

Submitted by Sam
Serves 4   **Serv/Size** 1 1/4 cups   **Cal/Serv** 250
Sodium 85mg   **Calcium** 70mg   **Cholesterol** 50mg
Fiber 5g   **Fat/Serv** 3g   **Fat** 12%

Exchanges: 3P, 1B, 1V

Sam's Note:
*Sauté means to rapidly cook so vegetables remain green and crisp. It is **not** the same as fry until limp.*

Chicken Tetrazzini

Marinate overnight in refrigerator:
4 boneless, skinless chicken breasts
2 cloves garlic, crushed
1/2 tsp. ground ginger
1Tbsp. vinegar
1/2 cup light soy sauce
1/4 cup white wine
Prepare according to package directions:
4 oz. dry angel hair pasta
Sauté mushrooms in microwave 1 minute:
1 1/2 cups fresh mushrooms, sliced

- **On medium heat, in non-stick saucepan, melt margarine with flour to make rue. Gradually stir in broth and milk, stirring constantly until thick. Add wine, seasonings and mushrooms.**

1 Tbsp. margarine	1 Tbsp. white wine
1/4 cup flour	1/4 tsp. pepper
1 cup chicken broth	1/4 tsp. poultry seasoning
1 cup evap. skim milk	

- **Preheat oven to 350°.**
- **Combine sauce and pasta, pour into a 7x11" baking dish. Top with chicken breasts.**
- **Sprinkle with 1/4 cup Parmesan cheese, grated.**
- **Bake covered 25 minutes.**

Submitted by Sharon Nelson
Serves 4 Serv/Size 1 breast - 1 1/4 cups pasta
Cal/Serv 390 **Sodium** 1500mg **Calcium** 200mg **Cholesterol** 55mg **Fiber** 2g **Fat/Serv** 9g **Fat** 15%

Exchanges: **4P, 2B, 1F**

Sam's Note:
When flour and margarine are heated together, a little ball is formed, which is called Rue. Cuisine 101.

Chicken Breasts with White Wine and Rosemary

1/2 cup green onions, chopped
4 boneless, skinless chicken breasts
4 tsp. rosemary, crushed
1/8 tsp. garlic powder
1/8 tsp. lemon pepper
2 tsp. parsley flakes
1/2 cup white wine

- Sauté onion in microwave 1 minute.

- Place chicken breasts in a 7x11" baking dish.

- Combine onion with rest of ingredients. Pour over chicken.

- Bake covered 20 minutes.

- Serve chicken on platter, spoon on sauce.

- Good chilled for lunch.

Submitted by Carol Dobitz
Serves 4   Serv/Size 1 breast   Cal/Serv 120
Sodium 70mg   Cholesterol 50mg   Fiber trace
Fat/Serv 2g   Fat 15%

Exchanges: 3P

Chicken Broccoli Rolls

1/4 tsp. garlic powder
1/4 tsp. rosemary
4 boneless, skinless chicken breasts, pounded flat
2 slices (2 oz.) Mozzarella cheese, halved
1 pkg. (10 oz.) frozen broccoli spears, thawed, drained
1/4 tsp. paprika
2 tsp. Parmesan cheese, grated

- Preheat oven to 325°.
- Combine garlic and rosemary. Sprinkle over chicken. Lay 1/2 slice cheese on each breast.
- Top with broccoli spears. Fold long edges of chicken breast over broccoli, secure with toothpick.
- Sprinkle chicken rolls on all sides with Parmesan and paprika. Place seam side down in a 7x11" baking dish coated with non-stick spray.
- Bake covered 25 minutes.

Submitted by Editor
Serves 4 **Serv/Size** 1 breast **Cal/Serv** 165
Sodium 160mg **Calcium** 165mg **Cholesterol** 60mg
Fiber 3g **Fat/Serv** 2g **Fat** 20%

Exchanges: 4P, 1V

*Sam's Note: This recipe is a wonderful. Just like our Gourmet Editor. If using **fresh** broccoli in the above recipe, microwave 3 minutes on high. Enjoy!*

Hammed-Up Chicken

4 boneless, skinless, chicken breasts, pounded flat
2 tsp. parsley, snipped
1/4 tsp. paprika
1/8 tsp. basil
2 oz. thin sliced ham
4 slices (4 oz.) fat-free Swiss cheese
1 small tomato, peeled, seeded and cubed
2 Tbsp. Parmesan cheese, grated

- Preheat oven to 350°.
- Stir together seasonings. Sprinkle on chicken.
- Divide evenly and place on each breast: ham, cheese, and tomato.
- Fold over side of chicken, secure with toothpick, place seam side down. Place in 7x11" baking dish coated with non-stick spray.
- Sprinkle with Parmesan.
- Bake uncovered 25 minutes.

Submitted by Sam the Ham
Serves 4 **Serv/Size** 1 breast **Cal/Serv** 170
Sodium 525mg **Calcium** 55mg **Cholesterol** 50mg
Fiber trace **Fat/Serv** 3g **Fat** 16%

Exchanges: 4P

Sam's Note:
Always pound chicken with a meat mallet to be certain that the middle and edges are the same thickness, or you'll end up with the center uncooked and the edges dry.

French Chicken in Orange Glaze

4 boneless, skinless chicken breasts, pounded flat
1/2 tsp. salt
1 medium onion, chopped
1/4 cup green pepper, chopped
1 cup fresh mushrooms, sliced
2 tsp. parsley, chopped
1 orange, peeled and sliced
Sauce:
1 can (6 oz.) orange juice concentrate
1 Tbsp. brown sugar
1 tsp. grated orange rind
2 tsp. cornstarch

- Preheat oven to 350°.
- Mix together sauce ingredients. Cook over medium heat, stir constantly until thickened.
- Salt chicken, place in 7x11" baking dish.
- Sauté onion and green pepper in microwave 2 minutes on high. Add mushrooms, sauté 1 minute longer. Top chicken with vegetables.
- Pour sauce over chicken.
- Bake covered 25 minutes basting twice.
- Sprinkle with parsley, garnish with orange slices.

Submitted by Marlene Rieger
Serves 4 **Serv/Size** 1 breast **Cal/Serv** 245
Sodium 490mg **Cholesterol** 50mg **Fiber** 2g
Fat/Serv 2g **Fat** 10%

Exchanges: 3P, 2Fr

Beth's Crunchy French Chicken

1 bottle (8 oz.) fat-free French dressing
1/4 cup green pepper, finely chopped
1 tsp. chili powder
1/2 tsp. onion powder
8 boneless, skinless chicken breasts
1 1/2 cups corn flakes, measure then crush

- Preheat oven to 350°.

- Combine first four ingredients. Dip chicken in dressing mixture. Place in a 9x13" baking dish coated with non-stick spray.

- Sprinkle corn flake crumbs on top of chicken.

- Bake uncovered 25 minutes.

Submitted by Beth Anderson
Serves 8   **Serv/Size** 1 breast   **Cal/Serv** 170
Sodium 375mg   **Cholesterol** 50mg   **Fiber** 0g
Fat/Serv 2g   **Fat** 10%

Exchanges: 3P, 1B

Chicken Breasts Mexicano

4 boneless, skinless chicken breasts
1 clove garlic, minced
1/2 cup chicken broth
2 Tbsp. red wine vinegar
1 tsp. chili powder
1 can (4 oz.) chopped green chiles
1/2 cup fresh cilantro **or** 2 Tbsp. dry cilantro
1 Tbsp. margarine

- Sauté chicken breasts in non-stick pan, remove chicken.

- Add next four ingredients, simmer 5 minutes.

- Add green chiles, simmer 2 minutes.

- Remove from heat, swirl in cilantro and margarine.

- Return chicken to pan, turn to coat. Simmer 20 minutes.

Submitted by Carla Hansen
Serves 4   Serv/Size 1 breast   **Cal/Serv** 145
Sodium 270mg   **Cholesterol** 50mg   **Fiber** trace
Fat/Serv 4g   **Fat** 20%

Exchanges: 3P, 1F

Sam's Note:
The margarine is important in this recipe or the sauce will be too harsh.

Chicken Burritos

4 boneless, skinless chicken breasts, cut in strips
1/4 cup lime juice, or Rose's Lime juice
2 green onions, sliced
1 cup light sour cream
1/2 cup plain non-fat yogurt
4 (9") flour tortillas
3 cups lettuce, shredded
Robbie's Salsa (see following recipe)

- Marinate chicken in juice 1/2 hour. **Do not** marinate too long or chicken will get stringy.

- Fry chicken and onions in non-stick skillet.

- Stir together sour cream and yogurt. Add to chicken, simmer until heated through, **do not boil.**

- Divide chicken evenly on tortillas. Fold edges over, place seam side down on plate.

- Surround burrito with shredded lettuce. Top with Robbie's Salsa and 1 Tbsp. sour cream.

Submitted by Robbie Daniels
Serves 4   Serv/Size 1 burrito   **Cal/Serv** 350
Sodium 490mg   **Calcium** 85mg   **Cholesterol** 60mg
Fiber 5.5g   **Fat/Serv** 7g   **Fat** 18%

Exchanges: 3P,   2B,   1V,   1F

Robbie's Salsa

2 cups tomatoes, seeded and chopped
1/4 cup green onions, sliced
3 cloves garlic, minced
1 Tbsp. green chiles, chopped
2 Tbsp. lime juice
1/4 tsp. salt
1 Tbsp. fresh cilantro, chopped **or** 2 Tbsp. dry (optional)

● Combine ingredients in bowl, mix.

Submitted by Robbie Daniels
Serves 4 **Serv/Size** 1/2 cup **Cal/Serv** 35
Sodium 600mg **Cholesterol** 0g **Fiber** 0g
Fat/Serv 0g **Fat** 0%

Exchanges: 1V

Sam's Italian Chicken Breast

4 boneless, skinless chicken breasts
1 jar (16 oz.) spaghetti sauce
2 cups cooked (4 oz. dry wt.) Vermicelli, Angel Hair or
Spaghetti
1 cup (4 oz.) Mozzarella cheese, shredded

- Preheat oven to 350°.

- Place chicken in casserole, pour sauce over chicken.

- Bake covered 20 minutes.

- Top chicken with cheese, bake 5 minutes or until cheese
  melts.

- Serve chicken on top of 1/2 cup pasta.

Serves 4   **Serv/Size** 1 breast   **Cal/Serv** 295
Sodium 700mg   **Calcium** 235mg   **Cholesterol** 65mg
Fiber 3g   **Fat/Serv** 8g   **Fat** 21%

Exchanges: 4P, 1B, 1V

Sam's Meal Idea:
Yummy! (of course it is, it's my recipe) Serve this with
toasted light bread spread with margarine and garlic
powder. Add a tossed salad.

Chicken Romano

4 boneless, skinless chicken breasts
1/3 cup flour
1 1/2 cups tomato juice
1 1/2 Tbsp. apple cider vinegar
1 1/2 Tbsp. sugar
1/2 tsp. garlic powder
1/2 tsp. oregano
1 tsp. basil
1 medium onion, chopped
4 oz. fresh mushrooms, sliced
1 cup (4 oz.) Romano cheese, grated
2 Tbsp. parsley, chopped

- Dredge chicken breasts in flour. Brown in skillet coated with non-stick spray.

- Mix next eight ingredients, pour over chicken.

- Sprinkle with Romano and parsley.

- Cover and simmer 25 minutes.

Submitted by Joetta Barnes-Weible
Serves 4   **Serv/Size** 1 breast   **Cal/Serv** 290
Sodium 580mg   **Calcium** 340mg   **Cholesterol** 78mg
Fiber 2g   **Fat/Serv** 10g   **Fat** 27%

Exchanges: 4P, 1/2B, 2V

Valley Chicken

4 boneless, skinless chicken breasts **or** 8 drumsticks
1/2 cup skim milk (calcium fortified)
2 cups corn flakes, measure then crush
1/2 pkg. (1.1oz.) or 1 pkg. (.4 oz.) dry ranch dressing mix
3/4 cup Parmesan cheese, grated

- Preheat oven to 350°.

- Coat a 7x11" baking dish with non-stick spray.

- Dip chicken in milk, place in baking dish.

- Mix dry ingredients, evenly sprinkle on chicken.

- Bake uncovered 25 minutes.

Submitted by Beth Anderson
Serves 4   Serv/Size 1 breast or 2 drumsticks
Cal/Serv 225   **Sodium** 475mg   **Calcium** 354mg
Cholesterol 62mg   **Fiber** 0g   **Fat/Serv** 6g   **Fat** 25%

Exchanges: 4P, 1/2B

Parmesan Chicken

1/2 cup Parmesan cheese, grated
1/4 cup whole wheat or white flour
1 1/2 tsp. paprika
pepper to taste
4 boneless, skinless chicken breasts
2 egg whites, slightly beaten
2 Tbsp. skim milk
Tabasco sauce (optional)

- Preheat oven to 350°.

- In a plastic bag combine Parmesan cheese, flour, paprika, and pepper.

- Beat egg whites and milk together. Add Tabasco.

- Dip chicken into egg mixture. Place pieces in plastic bag; close and shake to coat chicken. Place chicken in a 7x11" baking dish coated with non-stick spray.

- Bake uncovered 25 minutes.

Serve 4 **Serv/Size** 1 breast **Cal/Serv** 190
Sodium 270mg **Calcium** 160mg **Cholesterol** 60mg
Fiber trace **Fat/Serv** 5g **Fat** 20%

Exchanges: 4P

Oven Fried Chicken

4 boneless, skinless chicken breasts
2 egg whites
3 Tbsp. skim milk
Mix:
2/3 cup Parmesan cheese, grated
2 Tbsp. flour
2 tsp. paprika
1/4 tsp. pepper

- Preheat oven to 350°.
- Coat a 7x11" baking dish with non-stick spray.
- Place chicken in a plastic bag or between plastic wrap before pounding. Pound chicken flat with meat mallet. **Sam says "What the heck, for years I didn't have a mallet, I used my hammer".**
- Whisk together egg whites and milk. Dip chicken in mixture.
- Place chicken in dish, sprinkle with Parmesan cheese mixture. Let stand 10 minutes.
- Bake uncovered 25 minutes. Yummy!!

Submitted by Karlene Walls
Serves 4   **Serv/Size** 1 breast   **Cal/Serv** 185
Sodium 335mg   **Calcium** 210mg   **Cholesterol** 60mg
Fiber 0g   **Fat/Serv** 5g   **Fat** 25%

Exchanges: 4P

Sam's Note:
I would imagine by now you have figured out I want you to buy a 7x11" glass baking dish. C'mon, $5.00, treat yourself.

Crispy Fried Chicken

4 boneless, skinless chicken breasts
1 cup buttermilk
2 Tbsp. flour
1 cup corn flakes, measure then crush
1/2 tsp. thyme
1/2 tsp. marjoram
1/4 tsp. pepper
1/2 tsp. rosemary
1/2 tsp. salt
1/4 cup light mayonnaise

- Preheat oven to 350°.

- Soak chicken in buttermilk for 2 hours or overnight.

- Combine all dry ingredients.

- Place chicken in a 7x11" baking dish. Lightly coat top of chicken with mayonnaise. Sprinkle with dry ingredients.

- Bake uncovered 25 minutes, until golden brown.

Submitted by Kathy Halvorson
Serves 4   Serv/Size 1 breast   Cal/Serv 320
Sodium 850mg   Calcium 90mg   Cholesterol 60mg
Fiber 0g   Fat/Serv12g   Fat 34%

Exchanges: 3P, 1B, 2F

Sam's Note:
Did you buy that 7x11" baking dish yet?

105

Chicken Parisienne

4 boneless, skinless chicken breasts
1 can (10.75 oz.) cream of mushroom soup
1/2 cup plain non-fat yogurt
1 can (4 oz.) sliced mushrooms, drained **or**
1/2 cup fresh mushrooms, sliced
1/2 cup fine bread crumbs
paprika

- Preheat oven to 375°.

- Arrange breasts in single layer in 7x11" baking dish coated with non-stick spray.

- Combine soup, yogurt, and mushrooms. Pour over chicken. Sprinkle with bread crumbs and paprika.

- Bake uncovered 20 minutes.

Submitted by Pearl McCloskey
Serves 4   Serv/Size 1 breast   Cal/Serv 250
Sodium 875mg   Calcium 100mg   Cholesterol 50mg
Fiber 1g   Fat/Serv 8g   Fat 25%

Exchanges: 3P, 1B, 1F

Sam's Note:
Warning: if the recipe does not call for low-fat cream soup, DO NOT substitute it. Low-fat often contains too much water for the recipe.

Crispy Potato Chicken

4 Tbsp. Dijon mustard
1 clove garlic, minced
4 boneless, skinless chicken breasts
2 cups frozen hashbrowns
1 Tbsp. olive or cooking oil
Seasonings:
ground black pepper, parsley, cilantro, rosemary or chives

- Preheat oven to 350°.
- Mix mustard and garlic. Brush mustard mixture evenly on breasts. Place in a 7x11" baking dish coated with non-stick spray.
- Place hashbrowns in bowl, add oil. Toss.
- Top each chicken breast with 1/2 cup hashbrowns.
- Sprinkle with one or more seasonings.
- Bake 20 minutes. Broil five minutes if potatoes do not brown.

Submitted by Coleen Bitker
Serves 4   **Serv/Size** 1 breast - 1/2 cup potato
Cal/Serv 230   **Sodium** 590mg   **Calcium** 60mg
Cholesterol 50mg   **Fiber** 1.5g   **Fat/Serv** 6g   **Fat** 23%

Exchanges: 3P, 1B, 1F

Sam's Note:
I use a 1/2 measuring cup to place hashbrowns on chicken. This is a great recipe for the grill. Brown the chicken on one side, turn and add potatoes. Grill until potatoes are browned.

Sam's Mom's Turkey Casserole

4 cups cooked (8 oz. dry wt.) medium egg noodles
2 cups turkey, diced
1 can (4 oz.) sliced mushrooms, drained
1 can (15 oz.) asparagus pieces, drained
1 cup (4 oz.) light Cheddar cheese, shredded
1 can (10.75 oz.) low-fat cream of mushroom soup
1 can (8 oz.) evaporated skim milk **or**
1 cup skim milk (calcium fortified)

- Preheat oven to 350°.

- Combine the first five ingredients, stir gently being careful not to break up asparagus. Place in 2 quart baking dish coated with non-stick spray.

- Mix soup and milk. Pour and blend in casserole.

- Bake covered 35 minutes.

Submitted by Betty Ratzlaff
Serves 8   Serv/Size 1 1/4 cups   Cal/Serv 220
Sodium 480mg   Calcium 90mg   Cholesterol 30mg
Fiber 1.5g   Fat/Serv 2g   Fat 10%

Exchanges: 2P, 1B, 1V

Sam's Note:
*Since I can remember, my mother made this the day after Thanksgiving. **It's my favorite casserole!***

Chicken/Turkey Casserole

1 pkg. (6.75 oz.) regular and wild rice mix, **i.e.** Uncle Ben's
2 pkgs. (10 oz.) frozen broccoli
2 cups cooked chicken or turkey, cubed
1/2 cup light mayonnaise or salad dressing
1 can (10.75 oz.) low-fat cream of chicken soup
1 tsp. lemon juice
1 tsp. curry powder
1 can (6 oz.) water chestnuts, rinsed and drained
1 can (4 oz.) mushrooms, drained
1/2 cup (2 oz.) light Cheddar cheese, shredded
1/4 cup bread crumbs **or** crushed Corn Flakes/Wheaties

- Preheat oven to 350°.
- Cook rice according to directions, **eliminate margarine.**
- Rinse broccoli just to remove ice, cut in chunks.
- Place rice, chicken, and broccoli in 2 quart casserole coated with non-stick spray.
- Mix together remaining ingredients, except cheese and bread crumbs. Pour over chicken.
- Top with cheese and bread crumbs.
- Bake uncovered 25 minutes.

Submitted by Diana Lill
Serves 8   **Serv/Size** 1 1/2 cups   **Cal/Serv** 360
Sodium 1125mg   **Calcium** 100mg   **Cholesterol** 50mg
Fiber 4g   **Fat/Serv** 11g   **Fat** 27%

Exchanges: 2P, 2B, 2V, 1F

Turkey Lasagna

12 cooked lasagna noodles (do not overcook)
1 lb. ground turkey (no more than 10% fat)
1 medium onion, chopped
1 tsp. Italian seasoning
1 tsp. salt
1/4 tsp. garlic powder
1/4 tsp. pepper
2 cans (15 oz.) tomato sauce
2 cups (8 oz.) Mozzarella cheese, shredded

- Preheat oven to 350°.
- In non-stick skillet brown turkey and onion, drain. Stir in seasonings and sauce. Simmer 20 minutes.
- In bottom of a 9x13" baking dish coated with non-stick spray, arrange one layer of noodles 3 across. Top with 1/3 meat mixture and 1/3 cheese.
- Repeat ending with cheese.
- Bake covered 30 minutes.

Submitted by Bev Branstner
Serves 9   **Serv/Size** 1/9   **Cal/Serv** 370   **Sodium** 1110mg
Calcium 420mg   **Cholesterol** 50mg   **Fiber** 2g
Fat/Serv 10g   **Fat** 25%

Exchanges: 4P, 1B, 1V

Sam's Note:
Remember, when making a recipe using ground turkey, be sure to choose a package that states no more than 10% fat, or you may end up with the eyes, neck, beak and feathers! Ask your butcher to grind a fresh turkey breast for you instead!

Turkey Enchiladas

5 (8") flour tortillas
1 can (16 oz.) tomatoes, peeled and diced, drained
1 can (15 oz.) tomato sauce
1 cup green pepper, finely chopped
1/2 cup green onions, sliced
1/4 cup fresh parsley or cilantro, snipped
1 tsp. chili powder
1/2 tsp. crushed red pepper
1/4 tsp. ground cumin
8 oz. cooked turkey, chopped
1 pkg. (3 oz.) non-fat cream cheese, softened
1 cup (4 oz.) light Sharp Cheddar cheese, shredded, divided

- Preheat oven to 350°.
- Coat a 9x13" baking dish with non-stick spray.
- Heat tortillas. See **Sam's Note** below.
- In saucepan combine next eight ingredients. Bring sauce to boil, simmer 5 minutes.
- Combine turkey, cream cheese, 1/2 Cheddar cheese and 1/2 sauce.
- Spoon 1/5 turkey mixture onto each tortilla, roll. Place seam side down in dish.
- Bake covered 20 minutes.
- Pour remaining sauce on top, sprinkle with remaining cheese. Bake uncovered 5 minutes, or until cheese melts.

Serves 5 **Serv/Size** 1 tortilla **Cal/Serv** 295
Sodium 1280mg **Calcium** 260mg **Cholesterol** 38mg
Fiber 2.5g **Fat/Serv** 5g **Fat** 15%
Exchanges: 3P, 1B, 1V

Sam's Note: To warm tortillas, place flour tortillas between two damp paper towels, microwave 45 seconds. The fifth tortilla makes a great lunch.

111

Turkey Meatballs in Lemon Sauce

1 egg white, beaten
1/4 cup bran cereal
1 tsp. Worcestershire sauce
1 tsp. finely grated lemon peel
1 lb. ground turkey or beef (no more than 10% fat)
1/4 cup plain non-fat yogurt
1 Tbsp. cornstarch
1 Tbsp. lemon juice
1 small carrot, finely shredded
1 green onion, sliced

- Mix together first five ingredients, shape into 8 balls (approximately 1/4 cup each).
- Brown meatballs in non-stick skillet.
- Remove meatballs, cover, set aside.
- Combine yogurt, cornstarch, and lemon juice. Add to meat juices in skillet. Cook, stirring until thickened. **Don't boil or yogurt will separate.**
- Add carrots and onions, cook, stirring 2 minutes.
- Serve sauce over meatballs.

Submitted by Beth Anderson
Serves 4 **Serv/Size** 4 meatballs **Cal/Serv** 145
Sodium 135mg **Calcium** 50mg **Cholesterol** 50mg
Fiber 1.5g **Fat/Serv** 0g **Fat** 4%

Exchanges: 3P

Sam's Note:
This is a very healthy recipe. 3 proteins and 40 extra calories of good stuff.
Sam's Meal Ideas:
Serve over wild rice, with a green vegetable.

Turkey Rice Hotdish

1 lb. ground turkey **or** lean beef (no more than 10% fat)
1 small onion, chopped
1 cup rice
1 cup water
2 cans (10.75 oz.) low-fat vegetarian vegetable soup
pepper to taste

- Brown ground meat and onion, drain.

- In large skillet combine all ingredients.

- Cover, simmer 20 minutes.

Submitted by Connie Laude
Serves 4   **Serv/Size** 1 1/2 cups   **Cal/Serv** 220
Sodium 515mg   **Cholesterol** 55mg   **Fiber** 2.5g
Fat/Serv 2g   **Fat** 7%

Exchanges: 3P, 1B, 2V

Turkey Porcupine Meatballs

1 lb. ground turkey or beef (no more than 10% fat)
1/2 cup rice
1/2 cup onion, finely chopped
1/4 cup fresh parsley, chopped
1/2 tsp. garlic powder
1/8 tsp. salt
1/4 tsp. marjoram
1/4 tsp. thyme
1/8 tsp. pepper
1 tsp. chicken bouillon granules
1 cup warm water
1 can (16 oz.) tomato sauce
1 clove garlic, minced

- Preheat oven to 350°.
- Combine first nine ingredients in large bowl, stir well.
- Shape into 8 meatballs.
- Place in 2 quart casserole coated with non-stick spray.
- Dissolve bouillon in water, combine remaining ingredients, pour over meatballs.
- Bake covered 1 hour.

Submitted by Beth Anderson
Serves 4   Serv/Size 4 meatballs   Cal/Serv 190
Sodium 245mg   Calcium 110mg   Cholesterol 50mg
Fiber 4g   Fat/Serv 1g   Fat 5%
Exchanges: 3P,   1/2B,   1V

Sam's Note:
Remember! Read the ground turkey package. Companies still think we won't catch on. Just because the package states ground turkey, does not mean it is not 50% fat. You may be better off using lean hamburger.

Sam's Beef Stroganoff

1 lb. beef sirloin, cut in 1/4" strips
1 medium onion, sliced
1/2 tsp. garlic powder
1 can (4 oz.) sliced mushrooms, drained
2 tsp. Worcestershire sauce
1 can (10.75 oz.) low-fat cream of mushroom soup
1 Tbsp. cornstarch
1 cup plain non-fat yogurt

- In skillet brown beef and onion for 2 minutes, stirring once.

- Combine beef with next four ingredients. Cover, simmer 10 minutes.

- Mix cornstarch with yogurt, fold into beef. **Do not overheat or yogurt will separate.**

- Heat through.

Serves 4   **Serv/Size** 1 1/4 cups   **Cal/Serv** 230
Sodium 500mg   **Calcium** 130mg   **Cholesterol** 61mg
Fiber trace   **Fat/Serv** 7g   **Fat** 30%

Exchanges: 3P,   1/2B

Sam's Note:
Serve over 1/2 cup noodles, with a fresh tossed salad.

Burgundy Stew

1 lb. top or bottom round steak, cubed
2 carrots, sliced
1/2 cup celery, sliced
1 onion, sliced
1 can (8 oz.) thin sliced water chestnuts, rinsed and drained
1 1/2 Tbsp. tapioca
1/2 cup burgundy wine
1/2 cup fresh mushrooms, sliced **or**
1 can (4 oz.) sliced mushrooms, drained
1 can (16 oz.) whole tomatoes, drained
1 Tbsp. sugar
1 tsp. salt

- Preheat oven to 325°.

- Mix all ingredients in 3 quart casserole.

- Bake covered 1 hour.

Submitted by Sam
Serves 4   **Serv/Size** 1 1/4 cup   **Cal/Serv** 225
Sodium 870mg   **Calcium** 68mg   **Cholesterol** 51mg
Fiber 2.5g   **Fat/Serv** 5g   **Fat** 24%

Exchanges: 3P, 2V

Sam's Note:
Serve over 1/2 cup egg noodles.

Beef Burgundy

1 lb. boneless beef sirloin
1 Tbsp. cornstarch
1/2 cup water
1 medium onion, sliced in rings
1/2 cup burgundy
1 tsp. instant beef bouillon granules
1/8 tsp. thyme, crushed
1 bay leaf
dash pepper
1 cup fresh mushrooms, sliced

- Partially freeze beef, slice thin in bite-size strips.
- In non-stick pan cook beef until browned.
- Blend cornstarch in water. Add to beef along with remaining ingredients, except mushrooms.
- Simmer covered over low heat 20 minutes.
- Add mushrooms simmer 5 minutes.
- Remove bay leaf.

Submitted by Sam
Serves 4 **Serv/Size** 1 cup **Cal/Serv** 160 **Sodium** 118mg
Cholesterol 51mg **Fiber** trace **Fat/Serv** 4g **Fat** 28%

Exchanges: 3P

Sam's Meal Ideas:
Serve over 1/2 cup cooked rice or noodles, with
Cinnamon Baby Carrots, *and a fresh tossed salad.*

Brisket of Beef

3 lb. brisket (trim fat)
1 pkg. dry onion soup mix
1 can (16 oz.) whole cranberries

- Preheat oven to 325°.

- Place brisket on large piece of foil in a 9x13" baking dish.

- Mix soup and cranberries.

- Top brisket with mixture. Fold foil over brisket tightly, sealing ends.

- Bake 1 1/2 hours.

- Let cool, slice meat thin. Reheat in juice when ready to serve.

- May be made ahead of time and frozen.

Submitted by Carol Lieban
Serves 8   Serv/Size 3 oz.   Cal/Serv 410   Sodium 420mg
Cholesterol 115mg   Fiber 0g   Fat/Serv 16g   Fat 38%

Exchanges: 3P

Brandied Beef

1 tsp. paprika
1/2 tsp. basil
1/4 tsp. thyme
2 Tbsp. flour
1 lb. top or bottom round steak (cut in very thin slices)
1 clove garlic, minced
1 large onion, chopped
2 cups fresh mushrooms, halved
1/2 cup beef broth
1/2 cup brandy

- Mix first 4 ingredients. Dredge meat in flour mixture.

- Brown meat in non-stick skillet coated with cooking spray.

- Add rest of ingredients. Reduce heat to low, simmer covered 20 minutes.

Submitted by LeAnn Zogg
Serves 4   Serv/Size 1 cup   **Cal/Serv** 270   **Sodium** 144mg
Cholesterol 51mg   **Fiber** 1.5g   **Fat/Serv** 5g   **Fat** 22%

Exchanges: 3P

Sam's Note:
Serve over 1/2 cup egg noodles, and add a colorful vegetable such as frozen California Blend.

Crockpot Stew

1 lb. top or bottom round, cubed
1 medium potato, chunked
1 onion, cut in eighths
3 stalks celery, chunked
4 carrots, chunked **or** 1/2 pkg. (16 oz.) baby-cut carrots
1 bay leaf
1/2 tsp. basil
1/2 tsp. sugar
1/4 tsp. pepper
1 Tbsp. tapioca **or** 2 Tbsp. cornstarch **or** 1/4 cup flour
(optional for thickening)
1 can (16 oz.) stewed tomatoes

- Combine first five ingredients in crockpot.

- Mix seasonings and tapioca with tomatoes, add to crockpot

- Cook all day on low heat.

Submitted by Sam
Serves 4   Serv/Size 1 1/4 cup   Cal/Serv 225
Sodium 125mg   Cholesterol 50mg   Fiber 2g
Fat/Serv 5g   Fat 22%

Exchanges: 3P,   1B

Sam's Note:
Did you know every time you lift the lid on a crockpot steam evaporates, leaving food dry, and 15 minutes of cooking time is lost.

Beef Stew Hot Dish

1 lb. top or bottom round steak, cut in fourths
1 onion, sliced thin
1 can (4 oz.) whole mushrooms, drained **or** 8 oz. fresh
4 medium potatoes, sliced thin
1 can (10.75 oz.) low-fat cream of mushroom soup
1/2 cup skim milk (calcium fortified)
1 cup non-fat plain yogurt
1 cup (4 oz.) light Cheddar cheese, shredded

- Preheat oven to 350°.

- Place meat in a 9x13" baking dish. Top with vegetables.

- Mix together soup, milk, and yogurt. Pour over meat.

- Bake covered 1 hour.

- Remove cover, top with cheese, bake 10 minutes or until cheese melts.

Submitted by Cheryl Anderson
Serves 4   **Serv/Size** 1 1/2 cup   **Cal/Serv** 350
Sodium 935mg   **Calcium** 465mg   **Cholesterol** 87mg
Fiber 2.5g   **Fat/Serv** 9g   **Fat** 23%

Exchanges: 4P, 2B

Pepper Steak with Rice

2 Tbsp. cornstarch
1/4 cup beef broth
1/4 cup light soy sauce
1 cup rice
1 lb. top round steak
1 Tbsp. paprika
2 cloves garlic, crushed
1 medium onion, cut in chunks
2 green peppers, cut in chunks
2 large tomatoes, cut in bite size pieces

- Blend first three ingredients, set aside.
- Cook rice.
- While rice is cooking, cut steak in very thin slices. Sprinkle with paprika.   Marinate in cornstarch mixture for 10 minutes.
- Stir-fry meat 2 minutes in large non-stick skillet, remove meat.
- Stir-fry garlic, onion, and peppers 2 minutes, add meat and cornstarch mixture, stir until sauce thickens.
- Add tomatoes, stir gently.
- Serve over 1/2 cup rice.

Submitted by LeAnn Zogg
Serves 4   Serv/Size 1 1/4 cup steak-1/2 cup rice
Cal/Serv 245   Sodium 655mg   Cholesterol 50mg
Fiber 2.5g   Fat/Serv 6g   Fat 20%

Exchanges: 3P, 1B, 1V

Beef Oriental

1 Tbsp. cornstarch
1 Tbsp. light soy sauce
1 tsp. brown sugar
1 lb. boneless round steak, cut in thin strips
1/2 cup each: carrots, celery, and green onions, diagonally sliced
1/4 tsp. ground ginger
1 can (14.5 oz.) low-sodium beef broth
1 can (10.75 oz.) low-fat cream of mushroom soup
1 can (16 oz.) chinese vegetables, rinsed and drained **or**
2 cups fresh
2 cups cooked rice

- Mix first three ingredients, set aside.
- In non-stick pan, simmer raw vegetables and ginger in beef broth 5 minutes.
- Add meat, cook 5 minutes.
- Add cornstarch mixture, stir constantly until thick.
- Fold in soup and chinese vegetables, heat.
- Serve over 1/2 cup rice.

Serves 4   **Serv/Size** 1 1/4 cup   **Cal/Serv** 290
Sodium 610mg   **Cholesterol** 57mg   **Fiber** 3g
Fat/Serv 7g   **Fat** 22%

Exchanges: 3P, 1B, 1V

Sam's Note:
*I freeze my stir fry meats for **one** hour so they slice more easily. I also like to use my electric knife.*

Curry Beef Stir Fry

1 tsp. curry powder
1 1/2 tsp. sugar
1 Tbsp. cornstarch
1/4 cup beef stock **or** low-sodium beef broth
1/2 lb. round steak, cut into 1 1/2" strips
1 medium onion, quartered and cut in strips
1 small green pepper, cut in 1 1/2" strips
1 medium tomato, divided into 6 wedges

- Mix first 4 ingredients together, set aside.

- Stir-fry beef in non-stick skillet 1 minute.

- Add next 3 ingredients, stir fry 2 minutes.

- Add cornstarch mixture to meat, stir until sauce thickens.

- Serve immediately.

Serves 2 **Serv/Size** 1 cup **Cal/Serv** 195 **Sodium** 120mg
Cholesterol 50mg **Fiber** 2.5g **Fat/Serv** 5g **Fat** 26%

Exchanges: 3P, 1V

Sam's Note:
I like to serve this over cellophane noodles.

Salisbury Steak Burgers

1 can (10.75 oz.) low-fat cream of mushroom soup, divided
1 lb. lean ground beef (no more than 10% fat)
1/2 cup dry bread **or** cracker crumbs
1/2 tsp. salt
1/8 tsp. pepper
1 onion, finely chopped
1 egg white, beaten
1/3 cup water
1 pkg. (8 oz.) fresh mushrooms, sliced

- Preheat oven to 350°.
- Combine 1/4 of the soup with next 6 ingredients, mix well.
- Shape into 4 patties, arrange in single layer in an 8x8" baking dish coated with non-stick spray.
- Bake uncovered 20 minutes.
- Combine remaining soup and water, spoon over patties.
- Bake 10 minutes longer.
- Microwave mushrooms 4 minutes on high, garnish steaks.

Submitted by Pearl McCloskey
Serves 4   **Serv/Size** 1 patty   **Cal/Serv** 245
Sodium 735mg   **Cholesterol** 48mg   **Fiber** 1g
Fat/Serv 12g   **Fat** 46%

Exchanges: 3P, 1B

Sam's Note:
If you have any red wine available, pour 1/4 cup over mushrooms to sauté.

Meat Loaf

1 lb. lean ground beef (no more than 10% fat)
1 large onion, chopped
2 egg whites
salt and pepper
1 cup crushed saltine cracker crumbs **or** 1/2 cup oatmeal
1/4 cup skim milk (calcium fortified)
1/4 cup tomato juice **or** 2 Tbsp. ketchup

- Preheat oven to 325°.

- Mix all ingredients together, except tomato juice. Shape into loaf, place in loaf pan.

- Top with tomato juice.

- Bake covered 1 hour.

Submitted by Sam
Serves 5   Serv/Size 3 oz.-1/5   **Cal/Serv** 185
Sodium 448mg   **Cholesterol** 37mg   **Fiber** trace
Fat/Serv 9g   **Fat** 47%

Exchanges: 2P,   1/2B

Sam's Note:
The fifth serving is for a meat loaf sandwich the next day. Yum! Yum!

126

Reuben/Sauerkraut Meatloaf

1 lb. lean ground beef (no more than 10% fat)
1 oz. or 2 slices soft rye bread, cubed
2 large egg whites
1/2 cup fat-free thousand island dressing
1/8 tsp. pepper
1/2 tsp. caraway seeds
Filling:
1 can (8 oz.) sauerkraut
1 pkg. (2.5 oz.) corned beef
1/2 cup (2 oz.) Swiss cheese, shredded

- Preheat oven to 375°.
- Mix together first six ingredients.
- Press 1/2 mixture in loaf pan, make a slight indentation down center.
- Rinse and drain sauerkraut, pressing to remove liquid. Spoon on meat, top with corned beef slices and cheese.
- Top with remaining meat mixture.
- Bake covered 1 hour.

Submitted by Barb Holte
Serves 6   **Serv/Size** 4 oz.-1/6   **Cal/Serv** 205
Sodium 630mg   **Calcium** 110mg   **Cholesterol** 42mg
Fiber 1g   **Fat/Serv** 11g   **Fat** 49%
Exchanges: 3P, 1/2B

Sam's Note:
Meatloaf is very healthy! Please weigh it. Serve with a vegetable, 4 oz. baked potato, and 1 tsp. margarine. Total exchanges; 3 protein, 1 bread, 1 vegetable, 1 fat.

Stuffed Cabbage Rolls

12 cabbage leaves
2 Tbsp. vinegar
1 lb. lean ground beef (no more than 10% fat)
1 cup rice
1/2 tsp. salt
1 tsp. pepper
1 small onion, chopped
1 can (10.75 oz.) tomato soup, divided
Mix together and set aside:
remaining tomato soup
1 can water
pepper to taste
1/4 cup ketchup

- Preheat oven to 350°.
- Place cabbage leaves in kettle of water with of vinegar. Cook just enough to soften the leaves so they fold easy.
- Cook ground beef, drain.
- Mix next five ingredients with beef until well blended.
- Fill cabbage leaves with beef mixture, roll tightly, insert toothpick in folded edge to keep rolls together. Arrange in a 9x13" baking dish.
- Pour tomato soup mixture over cabbage rolls.
- Bake covered 1 hour.

Submitted by Sandy Koffler
Serves 6   Serv/Size 2 rolls   **Cal/Serv** 220
Sodium 545mg   **Calcium** 52mg   **Cholesterol** 36mg
Fiber 2.5g   **Fat/Serv** 9g   **Fat** 38%

Exchanges: 2P,   1/2B,   1V

Heavenly Hamburger

1 lb. lean ground beef (no more than 10% fat)
1 onion, chopped
2 celery stalks, sliced
1 can (16 oz.) Italian tomatoes, reserve liquid
1 can (2.25 oz.) black olives, sliced
1/8 tsp. salt
dash pepper
4 cups cooked (8 oz. dry wt.) egg noodles
1 cup (4 oz.) American cheese, shredded

- Preheat oven to 350°.

- Brown ground beef, drain.

- Microwave onion and celery on high for 3 minutes.

- Mix all ingredients together, except cheese.

- Pour in 3 quart casserole coated with non-stick spray.

- Bake covered 20 minutes.

- Stir in cheese, bake uncovered 5 minutes.

Submitted by Beth Anderson
Serves 6   **Serv/Size** 1 1/2 cup   **Cal/Serv** 320
Sodium 470mg   **Calcium** 160mg   **Cholesterol** 34mg
Fiber 2g   **Fat/Serv** 11g   **Fat** 32%

Exchanges: 3P, 1B, 1V

Three Bean Hot Dish

1 lb. lean ground beef (no more than 10% fat)
1/2 cup onion, chopped
1 can (15 oz.) kidney beans
1 can (15 oz.) butter beans
1 can (28 oz.) baked beans
1/2 cup ketchup
1 jar (2 oz.) real bacon pieces
1 tsp. mustard
1 Tbsp. vinegar

- Preheat oven to 350°.
- Brown ground beef and onion in non-stick skillet, drain.
- Mix rest of ingredients together. Combine with meat, place in roasting pan.
- Bake covered 1 hour.

Submitted by Karlene Walls
Serves 10   **Serv/Size** 1 cup   **Cal/Serv** 230
Sodium 920mg   **Calcium** 60 mg   **Cholesterol** 20mg
Fiber 6.5g   **Fat/Serv** 6g   **Fat** 23%

Exchanges: 2P, 1B

Sam's Note: Three bean Hot Dish is an old time favorite. It makes a complete meal, but as with all things portion control is important! Don't add brown sugar, there's already enough in the canned baked beans! !

Wild Rice Casserole

1 lb. lean ground beef (no more than 10% fat)
1 small onion, chopped
1/2 cup celery, chopped
1/2 cup wild rice, washed
1/2 cup white rice, washed
1 can (4 oz.) sliced mushrooms
1/4 cup light soy sauce
1 can (10.75 oz.) low-fat cream of mushroom soup
1 can (10.5 oz.) chicken rice soup

- Preheat oven to 325°.

- Brown ground beef, onion, and celery together in microwave 3 minutes on high, stir. Microwave 2 more minutes on high, drain well.

- Add remaining ingredients.

- Place in a 3 quart casserole, bake covered 1 1/2 hours.

Submitted by Renie Sinner
Serves 6   **Serv/Size** 1 cup   **Cal/Serv** 245
Sodium 1480mg   **Cholesterol** 30mg   **Fiber** 2g
Fat/Serv 9g   **Fat** 32%

Exchanges: 3P,   1B

Wild Rice Dish

1 lb. lean ground beef (no more than 10% fat)
1 medium onion, chopped
1 jar (2 oz.) real bacon pieces
2 cups cooked wild rice
1 can (10.75 oz.) low-fat cream of mushroom soup
1 can (10.75 oz.) low-fat cream of celery soup
pepper
garlic powder
May also add:
mushrooms
cooked celery
water chestnuts, rinsed and drained

- Preheat oven to 350°.

- Brown hamburger and onion, drain.

- Combine hamburger, bacon, and rice. Place in 3 quart casserole.

- Add soups, stir.

- Add pepper and garlic powder to taste.

- Bake covered 20 minutes

Submitted by Betty Witham
Serves 6   **Serv/Size** 1 1/4 cups   **Cal/Serv** 250
Sodium 620mg   **Cholesterol** 40   **Fiber** 2g
Fat/Serv 10g   **Fat** 37%

Exchanges: 3P, 1B

Spinach Lasagna

Brown and drain:
1 lb. lean ground beef (no more than 10% fat)
1 large onion, chopped
Mix and add to meat:
1 can (15 oz.) tomato herb sauce
1 can (6 oz.) tomato paste
3/4 cup water
2 tsp. parsley flakes
1 tsp. sugar
1 clove garlic, minced
2 tsp. basil
1 egg white, beaten
Mix together and set aside:
1 carton (16 oz.) fat-free cottage cheese
1 box (10 oz.) frozen chopped spinach, thawed, well drained
1 Tbsp. parsley flakes
1 tsp. oregano
Other ingredients:
8 oz. lasagna noodles, uncooked
2 cups (8 oz.) part-skim Mozzarella cheese, shredded

- Preheat oven to 350°.
- Coat a 9x13" baking dish with non-stick spray.
- Layer 1/2 noodles, meat sauce, and cottage cheese mixture, repeat.
- Bake uncovered 50 minutes. Top with mozzarella, bake 10 minutes. Let stand 10 minutes to set. Cut in 8 pieces.

Submitted by Sam

Serves 8   Serv/Size 1/8   **Cal/Serv** 265   **Sodium** 750mg
Calcium 250mg   **Cholesterol** 16mg   **Fiber** 2.5g
Fat/Serv 6g   **Fat** 20%
Exchanges: 3P, 1B, 1V

Sam's Note:
This recipe freezes beautifully after baking. Take out of freezer and pop right in the microwave. Great lunch for work.

Enchilada Casserole

1 lb. lean ground beef (no more than 10% fat)
3 Tbsp. dried onion
3/4 tsp. garlic powder
1 1/2 tsp. chili powder
1/8 tsp. cumin
1 can (10.75 oz.) tomato soup
1 1/2 cups tomato juice
6 corn tortillas, cut in 2" strips
1 1/4 cup (5 oz.) low-fat Cheddar cheese, shredded

- Preheat oven to 350°.
- Brown ground beef and onion, drain well.
- Mix next 5 ingredients with ground beef. Simmer 20 minutes.
- Alternate layers of tortillas and meat sauce in an 8x11" baking dish coated with non-stick spray.
- Bake uncovered 25 minutes.
- Sprinkle with cheese, bake 5 minutes longer, or until cheese melts.

Submitted by Dorothy Swenson
Serves 6 **Serv/Size** 1/6 **Cal/Serv** 206 **Sodium** 630mg
Calcium 55mg **Cholesterol** 27mg **Fiber** 2.5g
Fat/Serv 3g **Fat** 34%

Exchanges: 3P, 1B, 1V

Sam's Note:
It is worth your money to purchase a 7x11" or an 8x11" pan.

Taco Pie

1 lb. lean ground beef (no more than 10% fat)
1 pkg. taco seasoning
1 tube (8 oz.) crescent rolls
2 cups (8 oz.) light Cheddar cheese, shredded
Toppings:
shredded lettuce
diced tomato.
light sour cream
salsa

- Preheat oven to 350°.
- Brown hamburger with taco seasoning, drain.
- Line a 9" pie pan with crescent rolls.
- Fill pan with hamburger.
- Bake until crust is light brown.
- Spread shredded cheese on top, bake until cheese melts.
- Serve with toppings.
- Cut into 6 wedges.

Submitted by Francis Gallagher
Serves 6   **Serv/Size** 1/6   **Cal/Serv** 330   **Sodium** 1000mg
Calcium 275mg   **Cholesterol** 72mg   **Fiber** trace
Fat/Serv 19g   **Fat** 51%

Exchanges: 3P,   1HFB,   1/2F

Sam's Note: By mixing sour cream and salsa together, you can stretch the amount of sour cream used, and it is GREAT! (Drool)

Taco Casserole

1 lb. lean ground beef (no more than 10% fat)
1 onion, chopped
1 can (16 oz.) tomatoes, diced
1 can (10.75 oz.) tomato soup
1 can (16 oz.) kidney beans
4 tsp. chili powder
1/4 tsp. pepper
Topping:
1/2 head lettuce, shredded
1 cup (4 oz.) crushed taco chips
1 cup (4 oz.) light Cheddar cheese, shredded

- Preheat oven to 350°.

- Brown hamburger and onion, drain. Add next five ingredients.

- Place meat mixture in a 7x11" baking dish.

- Bake uncovered 30 minutes.

- Sprinkle toppings in order given.

Submitted by Karlene Walls
Serves 6 **Serv/Size** 1/6 **Cal/Serv** 345 **Sodium** 1170mg
Calcium 224mg **Cholesterol** 47mg **Fiber** 9g
Fat 13g **Fat/Serv** 34%

Exchanges: 3P, 2B

My German Pizza

1 lb. lean ground beef (no more than 10% fat)
1/2 onion, chopped
1/2 green pepper, diced
1/2 tsp. salt
1/2 tsp. pepper
1 bag (16 oz.) fat-free hashbrowns
3 egg whites
1/3 cup skim milk (calcium fortified)
1 cup (4 oz.) light Cheddar or Mozzarella cheese, shredded

- Preheat oven to 350°.
- Brown beef with next four ingredients.
- Place potatoes in a 9" pie pan coated with non-stick spray.
- Top with beef.
- Beat together eggs and milk, pour over beef.
- Bake uncovered 25 minutes.
- Top with cheese, bake 5 minutes or until cheese melts.
- Cut in six wedges.
- Reheats well!

Submitted by Joann Boyd
Serves 6 **Serv/Size** 1/6 **Cal/Serv** 195 **Sodium** 780mg
Calcium 180mg **Cholesterol** 47mg **Fiber** 1g
Fat/Serv 8g **Fat** 39%

Exchanges: 2P, 1/2B

Sam's Note:
Read the directions on the cooking spray can. Most people do not give the spray enough distance, therefore coating too heavily.

Ravioli

1 lb. lean ground beef (no more 10% fat)
1 medium onion, diced
2 Tbsp. sugar
2 cans (10.75 oz.) tomato soup
1 box (16 oz.) pasta of your choice
1 can (4 oz.) mushrooms, drained
2 cups (8 oz.) low-fat Cheddar cheese, shredded
2 Tbsp. Worcestershire sauce
3/4 cup corn flakes, measure then crush

- Preheat oven to 350°.

- Brown beef with onion in non-stick skillet, drain.

- Combine sugar and soup, add to beef mixture.

- Prepare pasta according to package.

- In 3 quart casserole, combine pasta, beef mixture, mushrooms, cheese, and Worcestershire sauce.

- Top with corn flakes.

- Bake uncovered 20 minutes.

Submitted by Ann Shook
Serves 6 **Serv/Size** 1/6 **Cal/Serv** 450 **Sodium** 988mg
Cholesterol 47mg **Fiber** 3.5g **Fat/Serv** 14g **Fat** 27%

Exchanges: 4P, 3B

Pizza Hot Dish

1 lb. lean ground beef (no more than 10% fat)
1 jar (8 oz.) pizza sauce
1 can (8 oz.) tomato sauce
1 tsp. oregano
1/2 tsp. garlic powder
1 can (4 oz.) sliced mushrooms, drained
1 pkg. (8 oz. dry wt.) wide noodles
1 can (10.75 oz.) Cheddar cheese **or** Nacho cheese soup
1 cup (4 oz.) low-fat Mozzarella cheese, shredded

- Preheat oven to 350°.
- Brown ground beef, drain. Simmer with next five ingredients for 30 minutes.
- Cook noodles, drain. Combine soup with noodles.
- Layer noodle mixture and ground beef sauce in a 9x13" baking dish coated with non-stick spray. Repeat.
- Bake uncovered 25 minutes.
- Top with cheese, bake 5 minutes or until cheese melts.

Submitted by Karlene Walls
Serves 8   Serv/Size 1/8   Cal/Serv 275   **Sodium** 565mg
Calcium 120mg   **Cholesterol** 30mg   **Fiber** 2g
Fat/Serv 11g   **Fat** 37%

Exchanges: 3P, 1B, 1V

Sam's Meal Ideas:
Serve with tossed salad and fresh fruit.

Spaghetti Hot Dish

1 lb. lean ground beef (no more than 10% fat)
1 large onion, chopped
1 jar (12 oz.) spaghetti sauce
1/2 pkg. (16 oz.) fine egg noodles
1 cup (4 oz.) light Cheddar cheese, shredded

- Preheat oven to 350°.

- Brown ground beef and onion, drain.

- Add spaghetti sauce, simmer 10 minutes.

- Cook noodles, drain.

- Combine noodles and sauce. Place in a 2 quart casserole coated with non-stick spray.

- Bake covered 25 minutes.

- Top with cheese, bake 5 minutes or until cheese melts.

- Can be made 1 to 2 days ahead and frozen.

Submitted by Karen Swift
Serves 6   **Serv/Size** 3/4 cup   **Cal/Serv** 260
Sodium 565mg   **Calcium** 160mg   **Cholesterol** 34mg
Fiber 2g   **Fat/Serv** 10g   **Fat** 34%

Exchanges: 3P, 1B, 1V

Waikiki Meatballs

1 lb. extra lean ground beef (no more than 5% fat)
2/3 cup bread crumbs
1/3 cup onion, minced
1 egg white
1/4 tsp. ginger
1/4 cup skim milk (calcium fortified)
2 Tbsp. cornstarch
1/4 cup brown sugar
1 can (8 oz.) pineapple tidbits, drained, reserve juice
1/3 cup vinegar
1 Tbsp. light soy sauce
1 medium green pepper, chopped
2 cups cooked rice

- Mix first six ingredients. Shape mixture by rounded tablespoons into 16 balls.
- In non-stick pan brown and cook meatballs. Remove from heat, keep warm.
- Mix cornstarch and brown sugar. Stir in reserved pineapple juice, vinegar, and soy sauce until smooth. Pour into skillet, cook over medium heat, stirring constantly until mixture thickens and bubbles.
- Add meat balls, pineapple tidbits, and green pepper; heat thoroughly.
- Serve over 1/2 cup rice.

Submitted by Sam
Serves 4   **Serv/Size** 4 meatballs - 1/2 cup rice   **Cal/Serv** 330
Sodium 313mg   **Calcium** 81mg   **Cholesterol** 42mg
Fiber 1.5g   **Fat/Serv** 11g   **Fat** 31%

Exchanges: 3P, 1B, 1Fr

Sam's Note:
These make a fantastic hors d'oeuvre. Makes 48 cocktail size meatballs.

Sukiyaki Meatballs

1 Tbsp. cornstarch
2 Tbsp. soy sauce
1 Tbsp. water
1 lb. lean ground beef (no more than 10% fat)
2 egg whites **or** 1/4 cup egg substitute
1/2 tsp. salt
1/4 tsp. pepper
1 medium onion, diced
1/2 cup celery, diced
1 can (14.5 oz.) low-sodium beef broth
1/4 tsp. sugar
1 can (16 oz.) bean sprouts, rinsed and drained **or** 2 cups fresh
2 cups cooked rice

- Mix first 3 ingredients, set aside.
- Mix ground beef with eggs, salt and pepper. Shape into 16 meatballs. Brown half at a time in a non-stick skillet. Remove, set aside.
- Sauté onions and celery in pan, stir constantly, until tender. Stir in beef broth, sugar, bean sprouts, and meatballs. Cover, simmer 15 minutes to blend flavors.
- Add cornstarch mixture to pan. Cook, until mixture thickens, stirring constantly.
- Serve over 1/2 cup rice.

Submitted by Ruth Greenmyer
Serves 4   **Serv/Size** 4 meatballs - 1/2 cup rice   **Cal/Serv** 250
Sodium 413mg   **Cholesterol** 40mg   **Fiber** 1g
Fat/Serv 11g   **Fat** 38%
Exchanges: 3P, 1B, 1V

Sam's Note:
The original recipe called for serving extra soy sauce to shake over meatballs and rice, plus 1/4 cup chinese noodles over each serving. If you choose to do this, the sodium will increase and 1/4 cup noodles add 1 Bread exchange=80 calories.

Chop Suey Hot Dish

1 lb. lean ground beef (no more than 10% fat)
1 small onion, finely chopped
1 can (10.75 oz.) low-fat cream of mushroom soup
1 can (10.75 oz.) low-fat cream of celery soup
2 cups water
1 cup instant rice
3 Tbsp. light soy sauce
1 can (4 oz.) sliced mushrooms, drained

- Preheat oven to 350°.

- Brown ground beef and onion, drain.

- Combine soups and water.

- Mix all ingredients in 2 quart casserole coated with non-stick spray.

- Bake covered 30 minutes.

Submitted by Geri Walz
Serves 6   **Serv/Size** 1 1/4 cup   **Cal/Serv** 210
Sodium 790mg   **Cholesterol** 36mg   **Fiber** 2g
Fat/Serv 9g   **Fat** 37%

Exchanges: 2P, 1B

Pork Chops and Rice

2 pork loin chops
1/2 cup rice
1 can (16 oz.) tomatoes, cut, diced and peeled
pepper

- Preheat oven to 350°.

- Place rice in a 7x11" baking dish, top with chops.

- Cover with tomatoes. Pepper to taste. (optional)

- Bake covered 1 hour.

Submitted by Mom Eukel
Serves 2   **Serv/Size** 1 chop-1/2 cup rice   **Cal/Serv** 200
Sodium 820mg   **Cholesterol** 36mg   **Fiber** 3g
Fat/Serv 9g   **Fat** 39%

Exchanges: 3P, 1B, 1V

Sauerkraut and Pork

1 can (32 oz.) sauerkraut
1 medium onion, chopped
3 Tbsp. brown sugar
pepper
4 center cut pork chop (fat trimmed)
1/4 cup water

- Rinse sauerkraut under warm water, squeeze dry.

- Mix sauerkraut with next three ingredients.

- In skillet coated with non-stick spray, brown chops.

- Spread sauerkraut mixture evenly on top of chops.

- Add water, cover and simmer 25 minutes. Baste once.

Submitted by Kathy Halvorson
Serves 4 **Serv/Size** 1 chop-3/4 sauerkraut **Cal/Serv** 195
Sodium 790mg **Calcium** 55mg **Cholesterol** 36mg
Fiber 2g **Fat/Serv** 10g **Fat** 42%

Exchanges: 3P, 1/2Fr, 1V

Easy Pork Chops

1/2 tsp. dry mustard
1 tsp. brown sugar
1 Tbsp. chili sauce
1 pork loin chop

- Preheat oven to 350°.

- Combine first three ingredients, spread over pork chop.

- Bake uncovered for 25 minutes.

- Great for **single** people!

Submitted by Susan Zimmerman
Serves 1   **Cal/Serv** 170   **Sodium** 240mg
Cholesterol 36mg   **Fiber** 0g   **Fat/Serv** 3g   **Fat** 16%

Exchanges: 3P

Jamaican Chop Suey

1 lb. pork loin, cut in thin slices
1/2 cup soy sauce
1 cup celery, chopped
1 can (10.5 oz.) chicken rice soup
1 can (10.75) low-fat cream of mushroom soup
1/2 cup water
1 can (4 oz.) water chestnuts, rinsed and drained
2 cups fresh mushrooms, sliced
1 large onion, chopped
1 can (16 oz.) chop suey vegetables, rinsed and drained **or**
2 cups fresh

- Preheat oven to 350°.

- Marinate pork in soy sauce 30 minutes.

- Combine all other ingredients in saucepan, simmer on low 20 minutes.

- Stir pork into sauce, place in a 9x13" baking dish.

- Bake covered 20 minutes.

Submitted by Doug Johnson
Serves 4   Serv/Size 1 chop-1/2 cup sauce   **Cal/Serv** 260
Sodium 1550mg   **Cholesterol** 63mg   **Fiber** 6g
Fat/Serv 6g   **Fat** 20%
Exchanges: 3P, 1B, 1V

Sam's Note:
Serve over 1/2 cup rice. 1 Bread=80 calories.

Hawaiian Ham

1 can (8 oz.) chunked pineapple, in own juice, reserve juice
3 cups cooked center cut ham, diced
1 medium onion, cut in rings
1 green pepper, cut in rings
1/2 cup raisins
2 tsp. dry mustard
1/4 cup brown sugar
1 Tbsp. cornstarch
1/3 cup vinegar
1 tsp. Worcestershire sauce
1 Tbsp. light soy sauce
2 cups cooked rice

- Preheat oven to 350°.
- Add water to juice to equal 1 cup.
- Place ham in 2 1/2 quart casserole, top with pineapple, onion, pepper and raisins.
- In saucepan, blend juice and remaining ingredients, **except rice**. Cook, stir constantly until mixture boils and becomes slightly thickened. Pour over ham.
- Bake covered 20 minutes.
- Serve over 1/2 cup rice.

Submitted by LeAnn Zogg
Serves 4   Serv/Size 1 1/4 cup sauce-1/2 cup rice
Cal/Serv 320   **Sodium** 1184mg   **Calcium** 80mg
Cholesterol 34mg   **Fiber** 2g   **Fat/Serv** 6g   **Fat** 16%

Exchanges: 2P, 1B, 2Fr

BBQ Ham

2 Tbsp. Worcestershire sauce
1 1/2 cups brown sugar
1/2 cup honey
juice of 1 lemon
1 jar (17 oz.) barbecue sauce
2 Tbsp. cornstarch
10 lbs. shaved lean ham

- Preheat oven to 275°.

- Mix first six ingredients, pour over ham.

- Bake covered 2 1/2 hours.

Submitted by Carol Leibham
Serves 50   **Serv/Size** 2 oz.   **Cal/Serv** 144
Sodium 915mg   **Cholesterol** 21mg   **Fiber** trace
Fat/Serv 4g   **Fat** 24%

Exchanges: 2P,   1/2Fr (comes from sugar and honey)

Sam's Ham

2 lbs. ham
1 can (17 oz.) yams
1 can (4 oz.) pineapple rings, in own juice
1/4 cup brown sugar
1 tsp. dry mustard
1 can (8 oz.) light pears, halved
1 can (8 oz.) light peaches, halved
1/4 tsp. pumpkin pie spice
12 cherries, halved

- Preheat oven to 350°.
- Place ham and yams in a 9x13" baking dish.
- Drain pineapple, reserve juice.
- Mix brown sugar, mustard, and 1/2 cup reserved juice. Pour over ham and yams.
- Combine rest of fruit with pie spice, set aside.
- Bake ham uncovered 1/2 hour.
- Drain fruit, place around ham.
- Bake 10 minutes.
- Serve ham on platter, **arrange fruit around ham says Sam the ham.**

Submitted by Sam
Serves 6   **Serv/Size** 4 oz. ham-4 oz. fruit-4 oz. yams
Cal/Serv 322   **Sodium** 1400mg   **Cholesterol** 36mg
Fiber 2g   **Fat/Serv** 6g   **Fat** 16%

Exchanges: 3P, 1B, 2Fr

Sam's Note:
This is one of my favorite traditional Easter recipes. It is easy and ready to be put in the oven when you get home from church.

Sam's Orange Roughy

1 (5-6 oz.) orange roughy filet
1 Tbsp. skim milk (calcium fortified)
2 tsp. bread crumbs
1 tsp. margarine, melted (optional; 45 calories/1 Fat)
1 tsp. toasted slivered almonds (optional; 45 calories/1 Fat)

- Preheat oven to 500°.
- Moisten fish with milk.
- Top with bread crumbs.
- Sprinkle lightly with melted margarine.
- Bake for 13 minutes.
- Add toasted slivered almonds, bake 1 minute longer.

Serves 1   **Cal/Serv** 145   **Sodium** 120mg
Calcium 60mg   **Cholesterol** 15mg   **Fiber** trace
Fat/Serv 5g   **Fat** 56%

Exchanges: 3P, 1F

Sam's Note:
Should you decide not to use the optional calories in this recipe, you will save 90 calories per serving. Exchanges would then be 3 Protein.
*For me it's worth the extra calories, **sometimes.** While dining out, are you saving calories by ordering fish or seafood?. **Always** order fish in the three boring ways we all know; baked, broiled, and poached; no fats.*

153

Cajun Shrimp Creole

1 can (16 oz.) stewed tomatoes
1 medium onion, chopped
1/2 tsp. pepper
1/2 tsp. chili powder
1 tsp. basil
1 bay leaf
1 lb. fresh shrimp

- Combine all ingredients except shrimp.

- Simmer on stove 5 minutes or until bubbly. Stir once.

- Stir in shrimp, simmer 5 minutes. **Do not overcook!**

- Remove bay leaf.

Submitted by Sam
Serves 4   **Serv/Size** 1 cup   **Cal/Serv** 125   **Sodium** 160mg
Calcium 70mg   **Cholesterol** 130mg   **Fiber** 1g
Fat/Serv 2g   **Fat** 10%

Exchanges: 3P, 1V

Sam's Note:
Fish is 50% water. If it is overcooked it will shrink and be tough. Cook fish until it becomes opaque. This dish is delicious served over rice.
1/2 cup = 1 Bread, 80 calories.

Shrimp Bake

1 large onion, chopped
1/4 cup green pepper, chopped
1 clove garlic, minced
1 cup rice
1 can (15 oz.) low-sodium chicken broth
1 can (16 oz.) diced tomatoes, with juice
1 tsp. oregano
1 lb. shrimp
4 tsp. real bacon pieces

- Preheat oven to 350°.

- Sauté first three ingredients in non-stick pan until tender. Add rice and blend well. Sauté until rice turns white.

- Place in casserole with broth, tomatoes, and oregano. Stir and cover.

- Bake covered for 20 minutes.

- Add shrimp and bacon. Bake covered for 10 minutes.

Submitted by Nancy Young
Serves 4   **Serv/Size** 1 1/2 cups   **Cal/Serv** 170
Sodium 700mg   **Calcium** 110mg   **Cholesterol** 130mg
Fiber 3g   **Fat/Serv** 3g   **Fat** 10%

Exchanges: 3P, 1B, 1V

Lemon Pepper Shrimp and Zucchini

4 cups zucchini, cut diagonally in 1/2" slices
1 lb. shrimp
1 1/4 tsp. lemon pepper seasoning
dash of white wine (optional)

- Heat zucchini in a non-stick skillet over medium-high heat, stirring frequently until tender. Remove zucchini.

- In skillet, cook remaining ingredients for 5 minutes, stirring constantly.

- Return zucchini to skillet and heat 1 minute.

Submitted by Barb Henderson
Serves 4   **Serv/Size** 1 cup   **Cal/Serv** 95   **Sodium** 130mg
Calcium 65mg   **Cholesterol** 130mg   **Fiber** 4g
Fat/Serv 2g   **Fat** 14%

Exchanges: 3P, 1V

Sam's Note:
Shrimp is only 25 calories per ounce. A very low-fat protein!
Sam's Meal Idea:
Serve with Wild Rice and Cinnamon Baby Carrots. Both recipes can be found in Side Dishes.

Szechwan Shrimp

1 lb. shrimp, medium or large (shelled and cleaned)
1/4 cup light soy sauce
1/4 cup dry sherry or chicken broth
2 scallions (green onion), cut diagonally
1 tsp. ginger powder or 2 tsp. freshly grated ginger
1 tsp. sugar
1 tsp. red pepper flakes

- Combine ingredients, stir until shrimp is well coated. Marinate in refrigerator 2 or more hours.

- Remove shrimp from marinade, stir-fry 3 minutes in skillet coated with non-stick spray.

Serves 4   **Serv/Size** 4 to 5 shrimp   **Cal/Serv** 75
Sodium 730mg   **Calcium** 50mg   **Cholesterol** 130mg
Fiber 0g   **Fat/Serv** 1g   **Fat** 12%

Exchanges: 3P

Sam's Note:
*Give me **easy**, and this recipe is. By choosing light soy sauce, we reduced the sodium by 320mg.*

Stir-fry Polynesian Shrimp or Chicken

Blend and set aside:
2/3 cup cold water, 1 Tbsp. cornstarch
Combine:
1/2 can (3 oz) pineapple juice **concentrate**, thawed
2 Tbsp. light soy sauce,
1 tsp. chicken bouillon granules
Meanwhile back in the garden:
2 cups carrots, julienne
1 pkg. (10 oz.) frozen pea pods, rinsed **or** 1/2 lb. fresh
2 green onions, sliced diagonally 1/2"
1 tsp. ginger powder or 2 tsp. freshly grated
1 clove garlic, minced
1 lb. shrimp **or** 2 chicken breasts, sliced thin
1 Tbsp. vegetable oil (I prefer olive oil in stir-frying)
In wok or fry pan:

- Stir fry vegetables, ginger, and garlic in 2 Tbsp. water for 1 minute. Remove.
- Stir fry shrimp or chicken in oil. Push to sides.
- Pour juice mixture in center of wok. Cook and stir until bubbly and thickened.
- Return vegetables to wok. Heat through.

Submitted by Sam
Serves 4   Serv/Size 1 1/4 cup   Cal/Serv 150
Sodium 700mg   **Calcium** 100mg   **Cholesterol** 130mg
Fiber 2.5g   **Fat/Serv** 5g   **Fat** 20%
Exchanges: 3P, 1Fr, 1V, 1/2F

Sam's Meal Idea:
Complete this meal with 1/2 cup rice. 1 Bread/80 cal.

Grilled Scallop Kabobs

1 can (14 oz.) pineapple chunks, in own juice
1/4 cup white wine or chicken broth
1/4 cup light soy sauce
2 Tbsp. lemon juice
2 Tbsp. parsley, chopped
1/2 tsp. pepper
1/4 tsp. garlic powder
1 lb. fresh scallops, medium or large
8 oz. fresh mushrooms
2 large green peppers, cut in chunks
8 cherry tomatoes, save until end to top each skewer

- Drain pineapple, reserve 1/3 cup juice.
- Combine juice and next six ingredients in shallow baking dish.
- Add pineapple, scallops and vegetables, except tomatoes. Toss and marinate in refrigerator 1 to 1 1/2 hours.
- If using wooden skewers, soak in water for a few minutes to prevent burning.
- Alternate marinated pineapple, scallops, and vegetables on skewers, top with a cherry tomato.
- Place kabobs 4 to 5 inches from hot coals, grill 10 to 12 minutes turning and basting frequently with remaining marinade.

Serves 4   **Serv/Size** 2 skewers   **Cal/Serv** 205
Sodium 1200mg   **Calcium** 60mg   **Cholesterol** 30mg
Fiber 3.5g   **Fat/Serv** 1g   **Fat** 6%
Exchanges: 3P, 1Fr, 1V

Sam's Note: When kabobing always leave an air gap between protein and vegetables to insure even cooking! Place a sheet of foil coated with non-stick spray on grill to prevent seafood or fish from sticking, or falling through the grate.

Spaghetti with Clams

2 cans (6.5 oz.) chopped clams with juice
1 Tbsp. olive or vegetable oil
1/2 tsp. pepper
1 tsp. oregano
2 Tbsp. basil
1 tsp. garlic powder
2 Tbsp. parsley, chopped
4 cups (8 oz. dry wt.) Fettucini **or** thin spaghetti, uncooked
1/2 cup Parmesan cheese, grated

- Drain and rinse clams, reserve juice.
- Combine juice and next six ingredients, simmer for 20 minutes.
- Cook Fettucini during last ten minutes of sauce cooking time. Drain.
- While Fettucini is cooking, add clams to sauce; simmer 5 minutes.
- Pour sauce over pasta, toss. Sprinkle with Parmesan cheese.

Submitted by Elly Holland
Serves 4   Serv/Size 4 oz. sauce/1 cup pasta/2 Tbsp.
Parmesan   **Cal/Serv** 315   **Sodium** 5600mg
Calcium 225mg   **Cholesterol** 20mg   **Fiber** 2g
Fat/Serv 8g   **Fat** 22%

Exchanges: 3P, 2B

Sam's Meal Idea:
Spinach salad would be a great accompaniment.

Seafood Fettucini

2 cups (2 oz. dry wt.) **cooked** Fettucini noodles

Microwave on high for 4 minutes:
1 pkg. (10 oz.) frozen chopped broccoli **or** 2 cups fresh, chopped
1/2 cup carrots, shredded
1/4 cup onion, chopped
1/4 tsp. thyme leaves

Prepare:
1 pkg. (.87 oz.) white sauce mix **with**
3/4 cup skim milk (calcium fortified)

Add to sauce:
1 tsp. dried parsley flakes
1/4 tsp. thyme
1/8 tsp. garlic powder
1/4 tsp. basil

Mix:
Sauce, vegetables, 1 cup (4 oz.) Monterey Jack cheese, shredded
and 12 oz. cooked shrimp or crab

Toss:
Fettucini and sauce.

Sprinkle with:
1/4 cup Parmesan cheese

Submitted by Sam
Serves 4 **Serv/Size** 1 1/4 cups **Cal/Serv** 375
Sodium 720mg **Calcium** 440mg **Cholesterol** 160mg
Fiber 4g **Fat/Serv** 12g **Fat** 3%
Exchanges: 4P, 1B, 1V

Sam's Note:
*A basic rule to remember when dining out, **do not** order a
white sauce. Red tomato based is by far the more healthy
choice. You would save 1260 calories by preparing this
recipe at home. This is one of my favorite recipes!*

Fish Creole

1 pkg. (16 oz.) frozen cod or other filets
1 can (16 oz.) tomatoes, diced
1 medium onion, diced
1 medium green pepper, diced
1/4 tsp. garlic powder
1 cup rice
1/2 cup water
1/2 tsp. paprika
2 Tbsp. parsley, minced
1/4 tsp. Tabasco sauce

- Preheat oven to 350°.

- Thaw fish slightly and cut in bite size pieces.

- Combine all ingredients in 2 quart casserole. Stir gently.

- Bake covered for 1 hour.

Serves 4 **Serv/Size** 1 1/2 cups **Cal/Serv** 175
Sodium 300mg **Calcium** 85mg **Cholesterol** 36mg
Fiber 5g **Fat/Serv** 1g **Fat** 5%

Exchanges: 3P, 1B, 1V

Filets in Sour Cream

1 lb. pike or bass filets
1/4 cup flour
1/2 tsp. salt
1/4 tsp. pepper
1/2 cup skim milk (calcium fortified)
12 Ritz crackers, crushed and toasted
1/2 cup light sour cream

- Preheat oven to 350°.

- Cut fish into serving size.

- In small bowl, mix flour, salt, and pepper; lightly coat fish.

- Arrange in single layer in baking dish.

- Pour milk over fish.

- Bake for 45 minutes.

- Spoon sour cream over fish and sprinkle with cracker crumbs.

- Bake 10 minutes.

Submitted by Nora Halvorson
Serves 2 **Serv/Size** 3 oz. **Cal/Serv** 170 **Sodium** 700mg
Calcium 125mg **Cholesterol** 55mg **Fiber** trace
Fat/Serv 7g **Fat** 30%

Exchanges: 3P, 1B, 1F

Baked Fish

2 lbs. fresh or frozen fish filets
1 egg
1 Tbsp. water
1/2 cup fine dry bread crumbs
1/2 tsp. salt
pepper to taste
sliced lemon and onion

- This recipe is great for northern, walleye, or perch.
- Preheat oven to 350°.
- Thaw fish if frozen. Rinse and pat dry.
- Beat egg and stir in water.
- Combine bread crumbs with salt and pepper or other fish seasoning. Dunk fish in egg mixture, coating both sides, roll in crumbs, coating evenly. Place in baking dish coated with non-stick spray.
- Bake on one side 4 minutes, or until brown. Turn, place lemons and onion slices on top of fish, bake 5 minutes longer.

Submitted by Nora Halvorson
Serves 4   **Serv/Size** 3 oz.   **Cal/Serv** 130   **Sodium** 445mg
Cholesterol 90mg   **Fiber** trace   **Fat/Serv** 2g   **Fat** 15%

Exchanges: 3P, 1/2B

Sam's Note:
Fish loses water weight when cooked. Even though you start with 2 lbs., baking removes almost half the ounces because of the water in the fish that is cooked away. Do not overcook fish or it will be dry.

Baked Flounder

1 cup tomato juice
1/2 cup fresh or 1 can (4 oz.) sliced mushrooms
1 tsp. lemon juice
1 small onion, quartered
pepper to taste
1 1/2 lbs. flounder

- Preheat oven to 350°.

- Place all ingredients, except fish, in saucepan and bring to boil. Lower heat and simmer 5 minutes.

- Place fish in baking dish, pour sauce over.

- Bake covered for 20 minutes, baste twice.

Serves 4   **Serv/Size** 3 oz.   **Cal/Serv** 105   **Sodium** 330mg
Cholesterol 45mg   **Fiber** 1.5g   **Fat/Serv** 1g   **Fat** 10%

Exchanges: 3P, 1V

Salmon Loaf

1 cup white sauce (see below)
1 can (16 oz.) salmon, drained
1 Tbsp. lemon juice
1 egg white, beaten
1/2 cup celery, chopped
1 cup dry bread crumbs

- Preheat oven to 350°.
- Prepare white sauce.
- Add lemon juice to salmon.
- Thoroughly mix all ingredients together.
- Place in loaf pan coated with non-stick spray.
- Bake covered 35 minutes.

Serves 4   **Serv/Size** 1/4 of loaf or 4 oz.   **Cal/Serv** 230
Sodium 760mg   **Calcium** 320mg   **Cholesterol** 30mg
Fiber 1.5g   **Fat/Serv** 10g   **Fat** 31%

Exchanges: 4P, 1B

Sam's Note:
Directions for White Sauce: 1 Tbsp. margarine,
1/4 cup flour, 1/4 tsp. salt, 1 cup skim milk (calcium
fortified). In saucepan melt margarine over low heat.
Blend in flour and salt. Add milk all at once. Cook
quickly, stir constantly until mixture thickens and
bubbles.

Skillet Tuna Patties

1 can (10.75 oz.) low-fat cream of chicken soup, divided
2 cans (6 oz.) water packed tuna, drained
1/2 cup corn meal
2 egg whites, lightly beaten
1/2 cup onion, chopped
1/2 cup skim milk (calcium fortified)
parsley, chopped

- Mix thoroughly: 1/2 can soup, tuna, corn meal, egg, and onion. Shape into 4 patties. Brown patties in non-stick skillet.

- Stir together milk and remaining soup, heat. Serve 3 Tbsp. soup over patties.

- Garnish with chopped parsley.

Serves 4   **Serv/Size** 1 patty   **Cal/Serv** 160
Sodium 600mg   **Calcium** 55mg   **Cholesterol** 40mg
Fiber 2g   **Fat/Serv** 2g   **Fat** 15%

Exchanges: 3P,   1B

Creamed Peas and Tuna

2 tsp. margarine
1 Tbsp. cornstarch
1 cup skim milk (calcium fortified)
1/2 cup frozen peas, thawed
1 can (6 oz.) tuna **or** salmon, drained
4 slices light bread (40 calories per slice)

- In saucepan melt margarine. Stir in cornstarch until ball forms.

- Add milk, stir constantly on medium high until thickened. Remove from heat.

- Add peas and tuna.

- Serve over toasted light bread two slices per person.

Submitted by Sam
Serves 2 **Serv/Size** 1 cup **Cal/Serv** 250 **Sodium** 790mg
Calcium 380mg **Cholesterol** 35mg **Fiber** 6g
Fat/Serv 5g **Fat** 18%

Exchanges: 2P, 1B, 1F

Tuna Bake

1 can (4 oz.) sliced mushrooms
2 Tbsp. onion, chopped
2 Tbsp. flour
1 1/2 cups skim milk (calcium fortified)
1 Tbsp. dry sherry
1/4 tsp. salt
1/8 tsp. pepper
1/8 tsp. ground nutmeg
2 cups cooked (4 oz. dry wt.) spaghetti **or** macaroni
2 cans (6 oz.) water packed tuna, drained and flaked
2 Tbsp. Parmesan cheese

- Preheat oven to 350°.

- Sauté mushrooms and onion for 4 minutes in non-stick pan.

- Add flour and cook 1 minute, stirring constantly.

- Gradually add next five ingredients. Cook until thickened, stir constantly.

- Mix pasta, tuna and sauce in 1 quart casserole coated with non-stick spray. Stir well and sprinkle with Parmesan cheese.

- Bake covered for 25 minutes until bubbly.

Serves 4 **Serv/Size** 1 1/4 cup **Cal/Serv** 250
Sodium 515mg **Calcium** 240mg **Cholesterol** 35mg
Fiber 2g **Fat/Serv** 3g **Fat** 11%

Exchanges: 3P, 1B, 1/2M

Low Fat Chile Relleno Casserole

1 cup evaporated skim milk
4 egg whites
1/3 cup flour
2 cups (8 oz.) Monterey Jack cheese, shredded
2 cups (8 oz.) low-fat Sharp Cheddar cheese, shredded
3 cans (4 oz.) chopped green chiles
1 can (8 oz.) low-sodium tomato sauce (or regular)

- Preheat oven to 350°.

- Spray an a 8x8" baking dish coated with non-stick spray.

- Beat together first three ingredients until smooth.

- Mix cheese together, reserve 1/2 cup for topping.

- Alternate layers of chiles, egg mixture, and cheese in dish.

- Pour tomato sauce over top layer, sprinkle with reserved cheese.

- Bake uncovered 1 hour.

Submitted by Patty Ryland
Serves 6   **Serv/Size** 1/6   **Cal/Serv** 285   **Sodium** 900mg
Calcium 630mg   **Cholesterol** 75mg   **Fiber** trace
Fat/Serv 14g   **Fat** 45%

Exchanges: 3P, 1B

Zucchini Crescent Pie

4 cups zucchini, sliced
1 cup onion, chopped
2 Tbsp. parsley flakes
1/2 tsp. salt
1/2 tsp. pepper
1/4 tsp. garlic powder
1/4 tsp. basil
1/4 tsp. oregano
3 egg whites, beaten
2 cups (8 oz.) Mozzarella cheese, shredded
1 can (8 oz.) crescent rolls
yellow mustard

- Preheat oven to 375°.
- Sauté zucchini and onion in microwave for 4 minutes, drain. Stir in next six ingredients.
- Combine egg whites and cheese. Mix together with zucchini.
- Separate crescents into 8 triangles. Place in ungreased 10" pie pan. Press over bottom and up sides to form crust.
- Spread with mustard.
- Pour vegetable and cheese mixture into crust.
- Bake uncovered 20 minutes. Let stand 10 minutes before serving. Cut in six wedges.

Submitted by Susan Trandem
Serves 6   **Serv/Size** 1/6   **Cal/Serv** 285   **Sodium** 735mg
Cholesterol 20mg   **Fiber** 3g   **Fat/Serv** 15g   **Fat** 45%

Exchanges: 2P,   1HFB,   1/2F

Asparagus Casserole

1 pkg. (10 oz.) frozen asparagus spears **or** 1/2 pound fresh
1 can (10.75 oz.) cream of mushroom soup
1/2 cup skim milk (calcium fortified)
1 can (8 oz.) water chestnuts, rinsed and drained
1/2 cup (2 oz.) low-fat Cheddar cheese, shredded

- Preheat oven to 325°.

- Cook asparagus, drain and set aside.

- Combine soup and milk, stir until blended.

- Using a 1 1/2 quart casserole coated with non-stick spray, layer half of each; asparagus, soup mixture, water chestnuts, and cheese. Repeat layers.

- Bake uncovered 20 minutes.

Submitted by Eileen Kaehler
Serves 4   **Serv/Size** 1 cup   **Cal/Serv** 135   **Sodium** 865mg
Calcium 275mg   **Cholesterol** 16mg   **Fiber** 1g
Fat/Serv 7g   **Fat** 44%

Exchanges: 1P, 1/2B, 1V

Spaghetti Squash

8" spaghetti squash
1 medium onion, chopped
2 medium garlic cloves, crushed
1/2 lb. fresh mushrooms, sliced
1/2 tsp. oregano
salt and pepper to taste
1/4 cup chopped parsley, dried or fresh
1 tsp. basil
dash of thyme
2 medium tomatoes
2 eggs, beaten
1 cup fat-free cottage cheese
1 cup (4 oz.) part-skim Mozzarella, shredded
1/2 cup fine bread crumbs
1/4 cup Romano cheese, grated

- Preheat oven to 375°.
- Slice squash in half lengthwise, scrape out seeds and loose strands. Place halves face down on a cookie sheet coated with non-stick spray. Bake 30 minutes, or until a sharp knife easily inserts into squash.
- Cool squash, scoop out insides leaving strings in tact.
- Sauté next eight ingredients for 3 minutes in microwave.
- Cut tomatoes in half, remove seeds, dice.
- Combine eggs, and cottage cheese, add Mozzarella and bread crumbs.
- Combine all ingredients, except Romano, place in a 7x11" baking dish coated with non-stick spray. Top with Romano cheese.
- Bake uncovered 40 minutes, Romano cheese will be golden.

Submitted Tami Buchholz, R.D.

Serves 6 **Cal/Serv** 165 **Sodium** 500mg
Calcium 246mg **Cholesterol** 17mg **Fiber** 1.5g
Fat/Serv 5g **Fat** 28%
Exchanges: 1P, 1/2B, 1V

Broccoli Lasagna

1 pkg. (10 oz.) frozen broccoli, chopped
2 cans (10.75 oz.) cream of broccoli soup
3 carrots, thinly sliced
1 large onion, diced
8 oz. fresh mushrooms, sliced
12 lasagna noodles
1 carton (15 oz.) fat-free cottage cheese
4 egg whites, beaten
2 cups (8 oz.) part-skim Mozzarella, shredded

- Preheat oven to 375°.
- Rinse broccoli to remove excess ice, drain.
- In 2 quart saucepan heat soup on medium-low, add broccoli cook 5 minutes or until warm.
- Microwave carrots and onion on high 3 minutes, add mushrooms, microwave 1 minute longer.
- Prepare noodles as label directs, drain. (Do not overcook)
- In bowl, mix cottage cheese and eggs.
- In a 9x13" baking dish, spread 1 cup broccoli sauce. Arrange half noodles over sauce; top with half cottage cheese mixture, all carrot mixture, half mozzarella, half of remaining sauce. Top with remaining noodles, cheese mixture, and sauce. Top with Mozzarella.
- Bake uncovered 25 minutes, or until top is light golden brown.
- Remove from oven; let stand 10 minutes for easier serving.

Carol Dobitz
Serves 8   **Serv/Size** 1/8   **Cal/Serv** 390   **Sodium** 955mg
Calcium 410mg   **Cholesterol** 31mg   **Fiber** 4g
Fat/Serv 10g   **Fat** 20%

Exchanges: 2P, 2B, 2V

Vegetable Lasagna

8 lasagna noodles, cooked
1 pkg. (10 oz.) frozen spinach, chopped
1 pkg. (16 oz.) frozen broccoli, carrots and cauliflower
2 cups low-fat cottage cheese
1/4 cup Parmesan cheese, grated
1 Tbsp. margarine
1 cup skim milk, (calcium fortified)
1 Tbsp. cornstarch
1 tsp. instant chicken bouillon
1 cup fresh mushrooms, sliced
2 bay leaves
1 tsp. basil
1 tsp. oregano
1/4 tsp. celery seed
2 cloves garlic, minced
1 tsp. dried thyme, crushed
1/2 cup (2 oz.) Mozzarella cheese, shredded

- Preheat oven to 350°.

- Microwave spinach in package 5 minutes or until thawed. Open one end of package and squeeze sides to drain excess liquid.

- Run water over frozen mixed vegetables to remove excess ice, drain.

- Mix cottage and Parmesan cheese, add spinach, set aside.

- In saucepan melt margarine, stir in milk and cornstarch until thickened.

- Combine mixed vegetables, bouillon, and all spices. Microwave covered on high 5 minutes, stirring once.

- Layer 4 noodles in a 9x13" baking dish coated with non-stick spray.

- Spoon half of vegetable mixture over noodles, top with half of spinach mixture. Repeat.

- Bake covered 30 minutes.

- Sprinkle with Mozzarella cheese, bake until cheese melts.

-

Submitted by Sam
Serves 9 **Serv/Size** 1/9 **Cal/Serv** 230 **Sodium** 465mg
Calcium 205mg **Cholesterol** 8mg **Fiber** 5g
Fat/Serv 5g **Fat** 18%

Exchanges: 2P, 1B, 2V

Venison Stroganoff

1 large onion, chopped
1 lb. boneless venison
1 can (4 oz.) sliced mushrooms **or** 8 oz. fresh
1 tsp. Worcestershire sauce
1/4 cup red wine (optional)
1/2 cup water
1 can (10.75 oz.) low-fat cream of mushroom soup
1 cup non-fat plain yogurt
1 Tbsp. cornstarch

- Sauté onion 2 minutes in microwave.
- Slice venison in very thin strips, removing all fat and connective tissue, place in large saucepan.
- Add onions, mushrooms, Worcestershire, wine and water to almost cover meat. Simmer covered until fork tender.
- Add soup; continue cooking over low heat until sauce thickens.
- Stir yogurt and cornstarch together, blend with meat. (Do not boil)

Submitted by Harry Moore
Serves 4   **Serv/Size** 1 1/2 cups   **Cal/Serv** 250
Sodium 610mg   **Calcium** 140mg   **Cholesterol** 75mg
Fiber 1g   **Fat/Serv** 4g   **Fat** 13%

Exchanges: 3P,   1/2B

Sam's Note:
Serve over 1/2 cup rice or noodles, 1 Bread=80 cal.

Duck Breast in Wine

2 (6 oz.) duck breasts
salt and pepper to taste
1/4 cup flour
1 Tbsp. margarine
1/4 cup Burgundy wine
1 can (10.5 oz.) chicken and rice soup
1/4 cup onion, chopped

- Remove bones from breasts.
- Dredge breasts in flour and sauté in margarine until golden brown. Salt and pepper.
- Add wine, soup, and onion. Cover, cook on low heat, 2 hours.
- Liquid should cook down so breasts are coated with thick gravy.

Submitted by Harry Moore
Serves 4   **Serv/Size** 3 oz.   **Cal/Serv** 185   **Sodium** 650mg
Cholesterol 65mg   **Fiber** trace   **Fat/Serv** 7g   **Fat** 39%

Exchanges: 3P,   1/2F

Pheasant in Mushroom Gravy

4 boneless, skinless pheasant breasts, cut in pieces
1/4 cup flour
salt and pepper
1 can (10.75 oz.) low-fat cream of mushroom soup (may add water if too dry)

- Preheat oven to 250°.

- Roll pheasant in flour seasoned with salt and pepper.

- Brown in skillet coated with non-stick spray. Remove to roasting pan.

- Add mushroom soup, bake 1 hour.

Submitted by Harry Moore
Serves 4   **Serv/Size** 1 cup   **Cal/Serv** 180   **Sodium** 475mg
Cholesterol 6mg   **Fiber** trace   **Fat/Serv** 1g   **Fat** 9%

Exchanges: 3P,   1/2B

Beer Braised Venison Roast

2 1/2 lbs. boneless venison roast
2 cloves garlic, slivered
1 cup beer
1 can (8 oz.) tomato sauce
1 Tbsp. instant beef bouillon granules
4 potatoes, peeled and quartered
2 large onions, quartered
1/4 cup flour
1 tsp. salt
1/4 tsp. pepper
2 Tbsp. parsley, chopped

- Preheat oven to 325°.
- Cut small slits in roast, insert garlic slivers.
- Combine next three ingredients, pour over roast. Marinate in refrigerator for 2 hours, turn once.
- Remove roast, reserving marinade. Line a 9x13" baking dish with foil. Place roast in dish, add potatoes and onions.
- Dissolve flour in marinade. Pour over roast and vegetables, salt and pepper, garnish with parsley, cover with foil.
- Insert meat thermometer through foil into thickest part of roast. Bake 2 hours, or until thermometer reaches 180°.

Submitted by Geri Walz
**Serves 8   Serv/Size 3 oz.   Cal/Serv 265   Sodium 690mg
Cholesterol 85mg   Fiber 1g   Fat/Serv 3g   Fat 10%
Exchanges: 3P, 1B**

Sam's Note:
The Curried Fruit recipe would be delicious as a side dish for wild game.

Scalloped Corn (The best)

2/3 cup cracker crumbs (12 crackers or 2 oz.)
1/2 cup skim milk (calcium fortified)
2 eggs, beaten
1 can (15 oz.) creamed corn
salt and pepper

● Preheat oven to 350°.

● Mix all ingredients together.

● Pour into a 2 quart bowl greased with margarine. Place bowl in a pan of water, place both in the oven. (This is so corn doesn't stick to bowl).

● Bake uncovered 1 hour.

Submitted by Betty Ratzlaff
Serves 6   **Serv/Size** 1/2 cup   **Cal/Serv** 120
Sodium 385mg   **Calcium** 154mg   **Cholesterol** 70mg
Fiber 2g   **Fat/Serv** 3g   **Fat** 22%

Exchanges: 1/2P,   1B

Sam's Note:
This is my mother's recipe and definitely a favorite of mine and my family.

Cinnamon Baby Carrots

2 cups (8 oz.) baby-cut carrots
1 Tbsp. brown sugar
1/4 tsp. cinnamon
1 tsp. margarine

- In saucepan, steam carrots (approximately 15 minutes). Drain.

- Place carrots back in saucepan. Toss with remaining ingredients over low heat until margarine melts.

Submitted by Sam
Serves 4   **Serv/Size** 1/2 cup   **Cal/Serv** 45
Sodium 40mg   **Calcium** 30mg   **Cholesterol** 0mg
Fiber trace   **Fat/Serv** 0g   **Fat** 11%

Exchanges: 1V

Sam's Note:
Even children will eat these carrots!

Vegetable Casserole

1 bunch broccoli, cleaned and cut in chunks
1 small head cauliflower, cleaned and cut in chunks
1 bag (16 oz.) baby-cut carrots
8 oz. Velveeta cheese
15 Ritz crackers, crumbled
2 Tbsp. margarine, melted

- Preheat oven to 350°.
- Steam vegetables.
- Melt cheese, mix with vegetables.
- Place in a 9x13" baking dish coated with non-stick spray.
- Mix crackers and margarine. Spread over top of vegetables.
- Bake uncovered 30 minutes.

Submitted by Jean Bassett
Serves 8   Serv/Size 1 1/2 cup   **Cal/Serv** 275
Sodium 780mg   **Calcium** 360mg   **Cholesterol** 36mg
Fiber 2g   **Fat/Serv** 22g   **Fat** 60%

Exchanges: 1HFP, 2V, 2F

Sam's Note:
This is a vegetable recipe you might want to save for special occasions! However, to all bad there is a good. Each serving contains 360mg of calcium which is the same as drinking one cup of skim milk.

Baked Garden Vegetables

1 Tbsp. margarine, melted
1/2 tsp. salt
1/3 tsp. sugar
1 Tbsp. tapioca
1/2 cup onions, sliced
1 cup carrots, sliced
1 small green pepper, cut in chunks
1 cup fresh **or** frozen green beans
1 cup fresh tomatoes, seeded and chopped **or**
1 can (16 oz.) tomatoes, peeled and diced

- Preheat oven to 350°.

- Mix first four ingredients.

- Place vegetables in 2 quart casserole.

- Gently combine all ingredients.

- Bake covered 30 minutes.

Submitted by Sam
Serves 6   **Serv/Size** 3/4 cup   **Cal/Serv** 50
Sodium 490mg   **Cholesterol** 0mg   **Fiber** 2g
Fat/Serv 1g   **Fat** 20%

Exchanges: 1 Serv   1V
2 Serv   1 1/2V, 1F

Sam's Note:
This recipe works great for late summer vegetables.
Substitute or add yellow squash and zucchini.

Zucchini Stuffing Casserole

6 cups zucchini, sliced
3/4 cup carrots, shredded
1/2 cup onion, chopped
1 cup non-fat plain yogurt
1 cup (4 oz.) light Cheddar cheese, shredded
1 pkg. (8 oz.) seasoned bread crumbs, crushed, divided
1 can (10.75 oz.) low-fat cream of chicken soup
1 Tbsp. margarine, melted

- Preheat oven to 350°.

- Sauté vegetables in microwave on high for 5 minutes. Drain excess water.

- Mix vegetables with yogurt, cheese, and 1 cup crushed bread crumbs. Place in a 9x13" baking dish coated with non-stick spray.

- Spread soup over top.

- Mix margarine and remaining crumbs, sprinkle over casserole.

- Bake uncovered 25 minutes.

Submitted by Carrie Witte-Johnson
Serves 8 **Serv/Size** 1/8 **Cal/Serv** 110 **Sodium** 430
Calcium 180mg **Cholesterol** 20mg **Fiber** 3.5g
Fat/Serv 4g **Fat** 22%

Exchanges: 1P, 1B

Sam's Wild Rice Casserole

1 cup wild rice, **or** 1/2 cup wild rice and 1/2 cup white rice
1 can (4 oz.) sliced mushrooms, with juice
1/2 cup celery, chopped
1/2 cup onion, chopped
1/2 cup green pepper, chopped
1 can (14.5 oz.) chicken or beef consommé (depending on the meat you serve)

- Rinse rice. Place all ingredients in casserole coated with non-stick spray

- Let stand 3 hours to soften rice.

- Bake covered 2 hours, at 350°.

Submitted by Sam
Serves 6   **Serv/Size** 3/4 cup   **Cal/Serv** 125
Sodium 430mg   **Cholesterol** 0mg   **Fiber** 2g
Fat/Serv 0g   **Fat** 3%

Exchanges: 1B,   1V

Sam's Note:
*This dish can be prepared the day before. Cover and bake for **1 hour**.*

Fried Rice

4 eggs
1 cup white rice
1 Tbsp. oil
2 cups water
3 green onions, chopped
1 can (15 oz.) bean sprouts, rinsed and drained **or;**
2 cups fresh bean sprouts
1 can (6 oz.) water chestnuts, rinsed and drained
12 oz. leftover cooked shrimp **or** chicken
1 can (4 oz.) sliced mushrooms, drained **or**
1 cup fresh mushrooms, sliced
2 Tbsp. light soy sauce

- Beat eggs.

- In large non-stick skillet, cook eggs over medium heat without stirring until set. Loosen eggs, invert skillet over cutting board to remove. Cut eggs into short narrow strips.

- Fry rice in oil until golden brown.

- Add water to rice, cover. Simmer until tender, approximately 20 minutes.

- Add remaining ingredients. Heat through.

Submitted by Francis Gallagher
Serves 4 · **Serv/Size** 2 cups **Cal/Serv** 300
Sodium 350mg **Cholesterol** 260mg **Fiber** 4g
Fat/Serv 10g **Fat** 30%

Exchanges: 3P, 1B, 2V, 1F

189

Confetti Rice

2 cups tomato juice
1 cup frozen mixed vegetables
1 cup instant rice
1/8 tsp. pepper

- In medium saucepan, combine juice and vegetables. Bring to a boil.

- Stir in rice and pepper, cover.

- Remove from heat. Let stand 6 minutes.

- Fluff with fork.

Submitted by Jean Donahue
Serves 4   **Serv/Size** 3/4 cup   **Cal/Serv** 110
Sodium 380mg   **Cholesterol** 0mg   **Fiber** 4g
Fat/Serv 0g   **Fat** 3%

Exchanges: 1B,   1V

Brown Rice Pilaf

1 cup brown rice
2 1/2 cups water
2 tsp. chicken bouillon granules
1/2 cup onion, minced
Optional:
1 jar (2 oz.) diced pimentos, drained

- In saucepan combine rice, water, and bouillon granules.

- Bring to boil, reduce heat, cover. Simmer 40 minutes or until liquid is absorbed.

- Sauté onion in microwave 2 minutes.

- Fluff rice with fork, stir in onion and pimento.

- Serve immediately.

Submitted by Wanda Lorch
Serves 4   Serv/Size 1 cup   **Cal/Serv** 185
Sodium 560mg   **Cholesterol** 0mg   **Fiber** 5g
Fat/Serv 2g   **Fat** 9%

Exchanges: 2B

Make-Ahead Holiday Mashed Potatoes

5 lb. potatoes, peeled
1 pkg. (8 oz.) fat-free cream cheese
3/4 cup light sour cream
salt and pepper to taste
skim milk

- Preheat oven to 350°.

- Boil potatoes, drain and mash.

- Blend together cream cheese, sour cream, salt, and pepper. Add skim milk to reach desirable consistency. Fold into potatoes.

- Place in a 9x13" baking dish coated with non-stick spray. Cover and refrigerate. May be prepared the day before.

- Bake covered for 30 minutes.

Submitted by Barb Holter
Serves 10 **Serv/Size** 1 cup **Cal/Serv** 175
Sodium 250mg **Cholesterol** 6mg **Fiber** 4g
Fat/Serv 1g **Fat** 5%

Exchanges: 1P, 2B

Sam's Note:
I like to use light sour cream rather than fat-free in this recipe. Light sour cream is only 5 calories more per 2 tablespoons. The consistency and taste of light sour cream is better in this recipe than non-fat.

Cheesy Potatoes

12 cups (32 oz.) hashbrowns
16 oz. Velveeta cheese
1 can (12 oz.) evaporated skim milk

- Preheat oven to 350°.

- Place hashbrowns in a 9x13" baking dish coated with non-stick spray.

- Microwave cheese and milk together until blended. Pour over frozen hashbrowns.

- Bake uncovered 30 minutes.

Submitted by Bev Branstner
Serves 8   Serv/Size 3/4 cup   **Cal/Serv** 245
Sodium 1285mg   **Calcium** 80mg   **Cholesterol** 31mg
Fiber 1g   **Fat/Serv** 8g   **Fat** 30%

Exchanges: 2HFP, 1B

Sam's Note:
Because of the amount of fat in the Velveeta cheese,
*these are **high fat** proteins.*

Deluxe Hashbrowns

1 can (10.75 oz.) potato soup
1/2 cup light sour cream
1 small onion, chopped
12 cups (32 oz.) frozen hashbrowns
1/2 cup (2 oz.) light Cheddar cheese, shredded
1/4 cup chives, chopped (optional)
parsley flakes
paprika

- Preheat oven to 350°.

- Combine first six ingredients in large bowl. Toss lightly until coated. **Don't stir** or hashbrowns will become mushy.

- Place in an 8x8" baking dish coated with non-stick spray. Garnish with parsley and paprika.

- Bake uncovered 30 minutes.

Submitted by Renie Sinner
Serves 6 **Serv/Size** 1 cup **Cal/Serv** 180
Sodium 830mg **Calcium** 118mg **Cholesterol** 22mg
Fiber 2g **Fat/Serv** 3g **Fat** 14%

Exchanges: 1/2P, 1B

French Fries

4 medium potatoes, peeled
2 egg whites **or** 1 Tbsp. oil

- Preheat oven to 425°.

- Cut potatoes into French Fries.

- Combine egg whites or oil, and potatoes in zip lock bag. Shake until fries are coated. Spread evenly on baking sheet.

- Bake 10 minutes until golden brown, turning once.

Submitted by Sam
Serves 4   **Serv/Size** divide evenly   **Cal/Serv** 95
Sodium 34mg   **Cholesterol** 0mg   **Fiber** 2g
Fat/Serv 0g   **Fat** 0%

Exchanges: 1B

If using oil the calories per serving are 120, the total fat is 3 grams and 25% fat per serving.
Exchanges: 1B,   1F

Sam's Note:
Permission granted to eat these French Fries!

Easy Pineapple Dessert

1 box (9 oz.) white Jiffy cake mix
1 pkg. (1 oz.) sugar-free instant vanilla pudding
1 1/2 cups skim milk (calcium fortified)
1 carton (8 oz.) fat-free cream cheese, softened
1/2 cup skim milk (calcium fortified)
1 can (20 oz.) crushed pineapple, well drained
2 cups Light Cool Whip
2 Tbsp. toasted coconut (optional)

- Preheat oven to 325°.
- Prepare Jiffy cake mix according to directions, bake in a 9x13" cake pan.
- Cool cake 25 minutes.
- Mix vanilla pudding and 1 1/2 cups skim milk, pour over cooled cake.
- Mix next three ingredients until creamy, spread on pudding layer.
- Frost with Light Cool Whip, sprinkle with coconut.
- Refrigerate overnight.

Submitted by Susan Zimmerman
Serves 12   **Serv/Size** 1/12   **Cal/Serv** 190
Sodium 350mg   **Calcium** 90mg   **Cholesterol** 0mg
Fiber trace   **Fat/Serv** 3g   **Fat** 16%

Exchanges: 1/2P, 1B, 1/2Fr, 1F

Pineapple Dream Pie

3/4 cup flaked coconut
1 Tbsp. margarine, melted
1 pkg. (1 oz.) sugar-free instant vanilla pudding
1 can (20 oz.) crushed pineapple, drained, reserve juice
1 envelope unflavored gelatin
2 Tbsp. lemon juice
1 cup Light Cool Whip

- Preheat oven to 325º.

- Combine coconut and margarine. Press in bottom and up sides of a 9" pie pan. Bake approximately 15 minutes until golden brown, cool.

- Prepare pudding, set aside.

- Add water to pineapple juice to equal 3/4 cup.

- In saucepan combine gelatin and juice mixture, stir over low heat until dissolved. Add lemon juice, chill until partially set.

- Whip gelatin mixture until fluffy, fold in pudding and pineapple.

- Pour pineapple mixture into pie shell. Garnish with Cool Whip.

Submitted by Julie Pitsenbarger
Serves 8   Serv/Size 1/8   Cal/Serv 130   Sodium 50mg
Cholesterol 0mg   Fiber 0g   Fat/Serv 5g   Fat 35%
Exchanges: 1Fr, 1F

Rhubarb Refrigerator Dessert

1/2 cup sugar
3 cups rhubarb, chopped
1 pkg. (.3 oz.) sugar-free strawberry Jello
1 pkg. (1 oz.) sugar-free instant vanilla pudding
1 1/2 cups skim milk (calcium fortified)
1/2 carton (8 oz.) Light Cool Whip
Crust:
2 cups crushed graham crackers
3/4 cup non-fat plain yogurt
1/2 tsp. cinnamon

- In saucepan pour sugar over rhubarb, let stand 1 hour.
- Simmer rhubarb until tender, stirring occasionally. Add Jello, mix until dissolved. Chill until syrupy.
- Mix pudding with milk. Fold in Cool Whip. Add cooled rhubarb. Blend.
- Mix crust ingredients together. Pour 3/4 of graham crust into a 9x13" cake pan.
- Pour rhubarb over graham crust mixture, sprinkle with remaining crust.
- Refrigerate overnight.

Submitted by Nancy Young
Serve 15   **Serv/Size** 1/15   **Cal/Serv** 75   **Sodium** 50mg
Calcium 87mg   **Cholesterol** 0mg   **Fiber** 0g
Fat/Serv 1g   **Fat** 15%

Exchanges: 1Fr

Strawberry Pie

9" baked pie shell, cooled
4 cups quartered strawberries, set aside 8 pieces
1 pkg. (.3 oz.) sugar-free strawberry Jello
1 pkg. (1 oz.) sugar-free instant vanilla pudding
2 1/4 cups water
Light Cool Whip for garnish

- Place strawberries in pie shell, set aside.

- Mix Jello and pudding with water. Heat to full boil, remove from stove.

- Pour over strawberries, chill.

- Garnish each pie slice with 1 Tbsp. Cool Whip, and 2 strawberry pieces.

Submitted by Tami Buchholz, R.D.
Serves 8   Serv/Size 1/8   Cal/Serv 145   **Sodium** 300mg
Calcium 55mg   **Cholesterol** 0mg   **Fiber** 2g
Fat/Serv 5g   **Fat** 32%

Exchanges: 1HFB, 1/2Fr

Sam's Note:
Choose only one high fat bread exchange per day.
High fat breads contain 1 bread and 1 fat. Each fat
exchange is 45 extra calories.

Sensational Strawberry Dessert

2 pkgs. (1 oz.) sugar-free instant vanilla pudding
3 cups skim milk (calcium fortified)
2 cups Light Cool Whip, divided
2 pkgs. (10 oz.) unsweetened frozen strawberries **or**
3 cups fresh
9" round angel food cake, tear in 1" pieces

- Prepare pudding with milk, fold in half of the Cool Whip.
- Layer half the cake, fruit, and pudding in a 9x13" cake pan, repeat layers.
- Thinly spread remainder of Cool Whip over top of cake.
- Let set 4 hours or overnight in refrigerator.
- Garnish each piece with a sliced strawberry before serving.

Submitted by Dorothy Swenson
Serves 12   **Serv/Size** 1/12   **Cal/Serv** 308   **Sodium** 540mg
Calcium 130mg   **Cholesterol** 1mg   **Fiber** 5g
Fat/Serv 2g   **Fat** 5%

Exchanges: 1P,   2B,   1/2Fr

Sam's Note:
This recipe is especially great with fresh fruit. Try strawberries, blueberries, and bananas for the 4th of July. This recipe can be cut in half and put into an 8x8" cake pan. The remainder of the Angel Food cake freezes well.

Strawberry Angel Dessert

9" round angel food cake
1 pkg. (10 oz.) unsweetened frozen strawberries, thawed **or**
3 cups fresh, cut in small pieces
2 pkgs. (.3 oz.) sugar-free strawberry Jello
3/4 cup hot water
3/4 cup cold water **or** ice cube method
2 cups Light Cool Whip

- Tear cake into bite sized pieces, combine with strawberries. Place in a 9x13" cake pan cake.

- Combine Jello with hot and cold water, refrigerate to slightly thicken.

- Fold together Jello and Cool Whip, pour over cake.

- Poke cake with a fork to allow some of the mixture to move to bottom of pan.

- Refrigerate.

Serves 12   **Serv/Size** 1/12   **Cal/Serv** 220   **Sodium** 335mg
Cholesterol 0mg   **Fiber** 2.6g   **Fat/Serv** 1g   **Fat** 6%

Exchanges: 1B, 1Fr

Sam's Note:
Use your imagination. What do you have in your home? Try fresh peaches with peach Jello, or fresh blueberries with blueberry Jello.

Pink Champagne Dessert

1pkg. (10 oz.) unsweetened frozen strawberries **or**
1 1/2 cups fresh, cut in half
1 carton (8 oz.) fat-free cream cheese, softened
4 pkts. Equal
1 can (20 oz.) crushed pineapple, drained
2 bananas, quartered and sliced
1 1/2 cups Light Cool Whip
walnuts (optional)

- Thaw frozen strawberries, cut in half.
- Mix together cream cheese and Equal.
- Combine all ingredients.
- Place in a 9x13" cake pan, freeze.
- Remove from freezer 1 1/2 hours before serving.

Serves 12   **Serv/Size** 1/12   **Cal/Serv** 145   **Sodium** 85mg
Cholesterol 0mg   **Fiber** 3g   **Fat/Serv** 1g   **Fat** 9%

Exchanges: 2Fr

Sam's Note:
Fat-free cream cheese does not work in all recipes! In the Pink Champagne Dessert it is great, and what a difference in fat! Whenever using fat-free cream cheese, the cheese must be room temperature or it will not mix smoothly.

Sam's Suggestion:
This recipe freezes well. If you do not want to use the whole 9x13" cake pan, use two 8x8" cake pans and keep one for a later time.

Fruit Yogurt Cream Pie

9" prepared graham cracker crust
2 cups sliced fresh fruit
1 envelope unflavored gelatin
1/4 cup cold water
1 cup fat-free cottage cheese
1 cup plain non-fat vanilla **or** lemon yogurt
4 pkts. Equal
1/2 tsp. vanilla extract
nutmeg

- Arrange fruit in crust.

- Combine gelatin and water, stir over low heat until dissolved.

- In blender combine next four ingredients, mix until smooth. Gradually add gelatin mixture, blending well.

- Pour over fruit, sprinkle with nutmeg.

- Cover, refrigerate overnight.

Submitted by Eileen Kaehler
Serves 8 Serv/Size 1/8 Cal/Serv 130 **Sodium** 140mg
Calcium 120mg **Cholesterol** 1mg **Fiber** 1g
Fat/Serv 2g **Fat** 13%

Exchanges: 1P, 1/2B, 1/2Fr

Light And Fruity Pie

1 pkg. (.3 oz.) sugar-free Jello (my favorite is blueberry)
2/3 cup boiling water
2 cups ice cubes
2 cups Light Cool Whip
4 cups sliced fruit (strawberry, kiwi and blueberries are a great combo)
9" prepared graham cracker crust

- Dissolve Jello in boiling water.

- Add ice cubes, stir until Jello thickens, remove ice with slotted spoon.

- Blend in Cool Whip and fruit.

- Spoon into crust, chill 2 hours.

Submitted by Elly Holland
Serves 8   **Serv/Size** 1/8   **Cal/Serv** 135   **Sodium** 24mg
Calcium 55mg   **Cholesterol** 0mg   **Fiber** 2g
Fat/Serv 4g   **Fat** 25%

Exchanges: 1B,   1/2Fr,   1F

Sam's Note:
I like to use prepared pie crusts. I can't tell the taste difference between prepared and homemade, and they can be lower in calories. Try shortbread or Oreo, they're great!

Apple Pie

Easy Press In Pastry Crust (see next recipe) **or**
9" pie crust, unbaked
5 cups apples, peeled and sliced
3 Tbsp. lemon juice
1/3 cup sugar
2 Tbsp. flour
1/2 tsp. ground cinnamon
1/4 tsp. nutmeg
2 Tbsp. chopped walnuts (optional)

- Preheat oven to 375°.

- Combine apples and lemon juice, toss gently to coat

- In separate bowl combine remaining ingredients.
  Spoon over apple mixture, toss to coat.

- Pour filling into pastry shell.

- Cover pie with an aluminum foil tent.

- Bake 50 minutes.

Submitted by Pat Hanson
Serves 8 **Serv/Size** 1/8 **Cal/Serv** 175 **Sodium** 75mg
Cholesterol 0mg **Fiber** trace **Fat/Serv** 6g **Fat** 30%

Exchanges: 1HFB, 1Fr

Easy Press-In Pastry

3/4 cup. flour
1 Tbsp. brown sugar
1/4 tsp. salt
3 Tbsp. oil
1 Tbsp. cold water

- Combine flour, sugar, and salt.

- Add oil, stir with a fork until crumbly.

- Add cold water, stir with fork until moistened.

- Press dough evenly over bottom and up sides of 9" pie pan.

Submitted by Pat Hanson
Serves 8 **Serv/Size** 1/8 **Cal/Serv** 90 **Sodium** 73mg
Cholesterol 0mg **Fiber** trace **Fat/Serv** 5g **Fat** 50%

Exchanges: 1/2HFB

Sam's Note
Should you choose to use this crust with the previous Apple Pie recipe, the exchanges are 1/2HFB, 1Fr.

Pumpkin Pie

3 egg whites and 1 egg
2 tsp. pumpkin pie spice **or;**
     1 tsp. cinnamon
     1/2 tsp. ginger
     1/4 tsp. cloves
1/2 cup sugar
1 can (18 oz.) pumpkin
1 1/2 cups skim milk (calcium fortified)
9" pie shell, chilled

- Preheat oven to 450°.

- Whisk eggs, add all other ingredients. Mix until well blended.

- Pour into pie crust.

- Bake 10 minutes, reduce heat to 325°. Bake for 30 minutes or until knife inserted in center of pie comes out clean.

Submitted by Sam
Serves 8   Serv/Size 1/8   Cal/Serv 210   Sodium 180mg
Calcium 165mg   Cholesterol 27mg   Fiber 2.5g
Fat/Serv 6g   Fat 25%

Exchanges: 1HFB, 1Fr

Sam's Note:
Leave off the crust and the exchange would be 1/2Fr.

Graham Cracker Crust

2 Tbsp. margarine
2 Tbsp. sugar
12 graham cracker sheets, crushed

- In microwave melt margarine.

- Stir in sugar, add crushed crackers, mix well.

- Spread in a 9" pie pan.

- Chill for 1 hour.

Serves 8   **Serv/Size** 1/8   **Cal/Serv** 110   **Sodium** 168mg
Cholesterol 0mg   **Fiber** 0g   **Fat/Serv** 4g   **Fat** 30%

Exchanges: 1B, 1/2F

Sam's Note:
I'm lazy, I buy my graham cracker crusts and I can't taste the difference, and it can be lower in calories.

Sam's Fruit Cobbler

2 cans (15.5 oz.) light sliced peaches
1/4 cup sugar
1 Tbsp. cornstarch
1/2 tsp. cinnamon
1/4 tsp. nutmeg
1 cup flour
2 tsp. baking powder
1 Tbsp. sugar
1/4 tsp. salt
2 Tbsp. margarine
1/2 cup skim milk (calcium fortified)

- Preheat oven to 350°.
- Drain peaches, reserve 3/4 cup syrup.
- In saucepan, blend syrup and next four ingredients. Heat, stirring constantly, until mixture boils. Stir in peaches.
- Pour into an 8x8" baking dish coated with non-stick spray.
- Combine flour, baking powder, sugar and salt. Cut in margarine until mixture becomes coarse. Add milk, stir to moisten. Drop 9 spoonfuls over fruit mixture.
- Bake uncovered for 15 minutes. Serve warm.

Submitted by Sam
Serves 9   **Serv/Size** 1/9   **Cal/Serv** 225   **Sodium** 280mg
Calcium 137mg   **Cholesterol** 0mg   **Fiber** 3g
Fat/Serv 2g   **Fat** 10%

Exchanges: 1B, 1Fr

Cocoa Crazy Cake

1 1/2 cups flour
1/2 cup plus 2 Tbsp. sugar
1/4 cup unsweetened cocoa
1 tsp. baking soda
1/4 tsp. salt
1 cup water
3 Tbsp. plus 1 tsp. oil
1 tsp. lemon juice
1 tsp. vanilla extract
2 Tbsp. powdered sugar

- Preheat oven to 350°.

- Combine all ingredients, except powdered sugar, in an ungreased 8x8" cake pan, stir well.

- Bake uncovered for 30 minutes. Let cool in pan on wire rack.

- Sift powdered sugar over cooled cake.

Submitted by Pat Hanson
Serve 9   **Serv/Size** 1/9   **Cal/Serv** 175   **Sodium** 170mg
Cholesterol 0mg   **Fiber** trace   **Fat/Serv** 5g   **Fat** 28%

Exchanges: 1 1/2B, 1F

Apple Cake

1 1/2 cups sugar
2 egg whites
1 tsp. vanilla
1 cup applesauce
1/4 cup oil
2 cups flour
1 tsp. cinnamon
2 tsp. soda
1 tsp. salt
4 cups chopped apples (peel if skin is tough)

- Preheat oven to 350°.
- Cream together first five ingredients.
- Mix together next four ingredients, add sugar mixture, blend.
- Fold in apples, pour in a 9x13" cake pan.
- Bake uncovered 1 hour.

Submitted by Barb Holter
Serves 12   **Serv/Size** 1/12   **Cal/Serv** 240   **Sodium** 270mg
Cholesterol 0mg   **Fiber** trace   **Fat/Serv** 5g   **Fat** 18%

Exchanges: 1B, 1 1/2Fr, 1F

Sam's Note:
Many times I stood at the kitchen counter having only a small sliver out of the cake pan, as if that sliver didn't have any calories. Then I realized I had slivered the cake into oblivion.
From a sliver, to a slice, to a slob.
P.S. You don't have to even out the row.

Caramel Sauce

2 Tbsp. cornstarch
1/2 cup brown sugar
1/2 tsp. salt
1 Tbsp. margarine
1/2 cup evaporated skim milk
1/2 tsp. vanilla
2 Tbsp. light corn syrup

- Mix together cornstarch and sugar.

- Combine all ingredients in saucepan.

- Bring to boil, cook and stir until thickened.

- This is great spooned over the Apple Cake recipe. Heat 1 Tbsp. of sauce and pour over each piece of cake before serving.

Serves 12 **Serv/Size** 1 1/2 Tbsp. **Cal/Serv** 64
Sodium 120mg **Cholesterol** 0mg **Fiber** 0g
Fat/Serv 0g **Fat** 8%

Exchanges: 1Fr

Sam's Baked Apple

apple
1 tsp. brown sugar
raisins
toasted slivered almonds

- Core apple, mix together remaining ingredients, fill center of apple.
- Microwave for 5 minutes.

For four or more:
- Preheat oven to 350°.
- Coat 2 quart casserole with non-stick spray.
- Core, and slice one apple per person.
- Mix 2 Tbsp. brown sugar, 2 Tbsp. raisins, and 2 Tbsp. toasted almonds.
- Toss all ingredients in casserole, cover.
- Bake 20 minutes.

Serv/Size 1 apple   **Cal/Serv** 130   **Sodium** 20mg
Cholesterol 0mg   **Fiber** 3.8g   **Fat/Serv** 2g   **Fat** 12%

Exchanges: 2Fr

Sam's Note:
Top with a tablespoon of Cool Whip, or serve with 1/2 cup light vanilla ice cream. Apples have lots of pectin so they will make a nice sauce on their own. They smell wonderful while baking!!

Peanut Butter Surprise

1 pkg. (1.4 oz.) sugar-free instant chocolate pudding
2 cups skim milk (calcium fortified)
2 Tbsp. peanut butter
4 Tbsp. Light Cool Whip
2 maraschino cherries, halved

- Make pudding as directed, add peanut butter, mix.

- Divide pudding into 4 parfait glasses.

- Top with cool whip and a cherry.

- By using **calcium fortified milk** you increase the calcium supply to a full milk exchange.

Submitted by Sam
Serves 4   Serv/Size 1/4   Cal/Serv 125   Sodium 355mg
Calcium 250mg   Cholesterol 2mg   Fiber 2g
Fat/Serv 3g   Fat 24%

Exchanges: 1/2B, 1M, 1/2F

Sam's Note:
To make instant pudding thicker and to prevent separating, combine the following in a blender: 1 cup milk, pudding, 2nd cup milk. Blend on high 2 minutes. Scrape edge of blender. Blend 2 minutes. Scrape. Blend 1 minute. Viola!!

All American Parfait

For each person:
1/2 cup light vanilla ice cream
1/2 cup strawberries
1/2 cup blueberries

- Scoop 1/2 cup light vanilla ice cream onto cookie sheet, freeze.

- Clean fruit, cut strawberries in half, combine with blueberries.

- To serve, place ice cream scoops in pretty glass bowl, cover with fruit.

Submitted by Mary Lynk
Serv/Size 1   **Cal/Serv** 135   **Sodium** 50mg
Calcium 90mg   **Cholesterol** 5mg   **Fiber** 2g
Fat/Serv 2g   **Fat** 12%

Exchanges: 1B, 1/2Fr

Nectarine Sorbet

4 ripe nectarines, peeled and sliced
1 cup orange juice
1/2 cup water
1/4 cup non-fat vanilla yogurt
2 tsp. sugar

- In blender process all ingredients until smooth.

- Place blender in freezer for 4 hours. Remove from freezer 2-3 times during freezing, blending each time.

- Keep frozen until ready to serve, blend before serving.

Serves 6 **Serv/Size** 1/2 cup **Cal/Serv** 70 **Sodium** 6mg
Cholesterol 0mg **Fiber** 2g **Fat/Serv** 0g **Fat** 5%

Exchanges: 1Fr

Lemon Yogurt over Fruit

1 carton (8 oz.) non-fat lemon flavored yogurt
1 tsp. grated lemon peel (optional)

• Combine and pour over fresh cut up fruit.

Serves 2 **Serv/Size** half **Cal/Serv** 50 **Sodium** 35mg
Calcium 300mg **Cholesterol** 0mg **Fiber** 0g
Fat/Serv 0g **Fat** 0%

Exchanges: 1M

Sam's Note:
This adds a real spark to the fruit. Serve this recipe
for a brunch side dish, or have on hand for a snack.

Cranberry Yogurt Parfait

1 can (8 oz.) whole cranberry sauce
1 cup plain non-fat yogurt
1/2 cup (2 oz.) granola

- Divide evenly and layer ingredients in 4 Parfait glasses, ending with granola.

Submitted by Jean Donahue
Serves 4   **Cal/Serv** 175   **Sodium** 70mg   **Calcium** 130mg
Cholesterol 0mg   **Fiber** 0g   **Fat/Serv** 3g   **Fat** 14%

Exchanges: 1/2B,   1Fr,   1/2F

Cherries Jubilee

1 1/4 cups cold skim milk (calcium fortified) (brrrrr)
1/2 tsp. almond extract, divided
1 pkg. (1 oz.) sugar-free instant vanilla pudding
2 Tbsp. toasted slivered almonds, divided
1 cup Light Cool Whip
1 can (20 oz.) light cherry pie filling

- Pour milk, 1/4 tsp. almond extract, and pudding into bowl. Beat until blended.

- Gently stir in half the slivered almonds and Cool Whip.

- Mix cherry pie filling with remaining 1/4 tsp. almond extract.

- Alternate pudding and pie filling mixtures in 6 parfait glasses.

- Refrigerate until served. Sprinkle with remaining almonds.

Serves 6   **Serv/Size** 3/4 cup   **Cal/Serv** 140
Sodium 240mg   **Calcium** 120mg   **Cholesterol** mg
Fiber trace   **Fat/Serv** 2g   **Fat** 14%

Exchanges: 1/2M,   1Fr

Sam's Note:
This is a great recipe for my clients who have a difficult time eating all their fruits!

Cherries in the Snow

6 egg whites
1/2 tsp. cream of tarter
1/4 tsp. salt
1/4 cup sugar
1 tsp. vanilla extract
Filling:
1 carton (8 oz.) fat-free cream cheese
4 pkts. Equal
1 tsp. vanilla extract
2 cups Light Cool Whip
2 cups mini marshmallows
Topping:
1/2 can (20 oz.) light cherry pie filling
1/2 tsp. almond extract

- Preheat oven to 400°.
- Beat first three ingredients until stiff.
- Add sugar and vanilla, beat again.
- Spread in a 9x13" cake pan coated with non-stick spray, place in oven and turn heat off. Leave in oven overnight or 8 hours.
- Cream together next four ingredients. Add marshmallows. Spread on meringue.
- Chill 8 hours.
- Combine cherries and almond extract, spoon over each piece of meringue.

Submitted by Mavis Tjon
Serves 12   **Serv/Size** 1/12   **Cal/Serv** 120   **Sodium** 175mg
Cholesterol 0mg   **Fiber** trace   **Fat/Serv** 1g   **Fat** 10%

Exchanges: 2Fr

Old Fashioned Rice Pudding

2 cups skim milk (calcium fortified)
1/2 tsp. vanilla
1 cup rice
1/4 cup raisins
1/4 tsp. salt

- Preheat oven to 350°.

- Combine all ingredients. Pour into 2 quart casserole.

- Bake covered 1 hour.

- Sprinkle with Equal to taste.

Submitted by Sam
Serves 4 **Serv/Size** 1 cup **Cal/Serv** 140
Sodium 150mg **Calcium** 270mg **Cholesterol** 2mg
Fiber 2g **Fat/Serv** 0g **Fat** 3%

Exchanges: 1B, 1/2 M

Bread Pudding

2 eggs plus 2 egg whites
1 1/2 cups skim milk (calcium fortified)
2 Tbsp. honey
1 tsp. vanilla
1/2 tsp. cinnamon
1/4 tsp. salt
8 slices light bread, or 4 regular slices, cubed (use dried out bread, so bread doesn't get mushy)
1/4 cup raisins

- Preheat oven to 325°.

- Beat eggs until foamy. Add next five ingredients. Stir in bread cubes and raisins.

- Pour in 1 1/2 quart casserole coated with non-stick spray.

- Bake 40 minutes or until a knife inserted in center comes out clean. Most people prefer bread pudding served warm.

Submitted by Coleen Bitker
Serves 4 **Serv/Size** 3/4 cup **Cal/Serv** 220
Sodium 430mg **Calcium** 153mg **Cholesterol** 110mg
Fiber 5g **Fat/Serv** 4g **Fat** 14%

Exchanges: 1/2P, 2B

Banana Bread

1 cup sugar
1/2 cup margarine **or** 1/2 cup unsweetened applesauce
1 tsp. vanilla
2 eggs
3 bananas
2 cups flour
1 tsp. soda

- Preheat oven to 350°.
- Cream sugar, margarine and vanilla.
- Beat eggs. Mash bananas. Add both to sugar mixture.
- Sift flour and soda.
- Combine all ingredients, pour into lightly greased bread pan.
- Bake uncovered for 1 hour.
- While bread is warm, tip pan onto side, remove bread.

Submitted by Ruth Greenmyer
Serves 20 **Serv/Size** 1 oz. **Cal/Serv** 128
Sodium 92mg **Cholesterol** 21mg **Fiber** 0g
Fat/Serv 4g **Fat** 25%

Exchanges: 1HFB

Sam's Note:
*If you made this recipe with 1/2 cup applesauce instead of the margarine, you would save nearly **40 calories per slice**, that is **one fat**. Here is the nutrition analysis using the applesauce: **Cal/Serv** 105 **Sodium** 50mg **Cholesterol** 20mg **Fiber** 1g **Fat/Serv** trace **Fat** 6% **Exchanges:** 1B*

Blueberry Muffins

1 1/2 cups flour
3/4 cup sugar
2 tsp. baking powder
1 tsp. baking soda
1/2 tsp. salt
1 container (8 oz.) non-fat plain yogurt
1/3 cup skim milk (calcium fortified)
1/2 cup blueberries **or** grated apples

- Preheat oven to 400°.

- Combine first five ingredients.

- Blend yogurt and milk, add to dry ingredients. Mix until moistened, stir in fruit.

- Fill paper lined muffin cups 3/4 full.

- Bake for 18 minutes.

- **Light Streusel variation:** combine 1/3 cup sugar and 1/2 tsp. cinnamon. Fill muffin cups half full with muffin batter. Place 1 tsp. of sugar cinnamon mixture on top. Add batter to fill cups 3/4 full. 1 teaspoon topping = 15 calories.

Submitted by JoAnn Moody
Serves 12 **Serv/Size** 1 muffin **Cal/Serv** 110
Sodium 250mg **Calcium** 90mg **Cholesterol** 0mg
Fiber 0g **Fat/Serv** 0g **Fat** 1%

Exchanges: 1B

Seven Week Bran Muffins

1 cup 40% bran flakes cereal
1 cup boiling water
1/2 cup shortening **or** margarine
1 1/2 cups sugar
2 eggs plus 2 egg whites
2 cups buttermilk
2 1/2 cups flour
1/2 tsp. salt
2 1/2 tsp. baking soda
2 cups All-Bran cereal

- Preheat oven to 400°.
- Soak bran flakes in water, cool.
- Cream together shortening, sugar and eggs. Add buttermilk and bran flakes, mix until fluffy.
- Sift in flour, salt, soda. Add All-Bran, mix again.
- Refrigerate dough until ready to bake. **Guess how long this recipe keeps.***
- Bake for 12 minutes.

Submitted by Kim Peterson
Serves 48 (mini-muffins)   Serv/Size 1 muffin
Cal/Serv 80   **Sodium** 100mg   **Cholesterol** 10mg
Fiber trace   **Fat/Serv** 2g   **Fat** 27%
Exchanges: 1B

Sam's Note:
*2 mini-muffins would equal **2 Breads**. Think about the giant muffins you can order in restaurants.*
***1000 calories**=8 breads, plus 8 fat exchanges. I actually have clients who believe this is only 2 breads. Talk about denial.*   *7 weeks.*

Raspberry Bran Muffins

2 1/2 cups flour
1 3/4 cups sugar
2 tsp. baking powder
1/2 tsp. baking soda
1/2 tsp. salt
8 cups bran flakes cereal
2 cups buttermilk
1/2 cup applesauce
1 egg and 2 egg whites
1/2 cup raspberry fruit spread (20 calories per Tbsp.)

- Preheat oven to 350°.
- Combine first five ingredients, add cereal.
- In separate bowl, whisk together buttermilk, applesauce, and eggs. Add to dry ingredients, stir until moist.
- Spoon 1/4 cup batter into each muffin cup. Drop 1 tsp. raspberry fruit spread on top. Spoon 1/4 cup batter over jam.
- Bake 25 minutes.

Submitted by Becca Schmidt
Serves 24   **Serv/Size** 1 muffin   **Cal/Serv** 200
Sodium 290mg   **Calcium** 65mg   **Cholesterol** 10mg
Fiber 4g   **Fat/Serv** 0g   **Fat** 2%

Exchanges: 2B

Sam's Note:
This recipe is a great example of a weight gain, if all you think about is fat grams.

Breakfast

Dips and Drinks

Soups and Sam'iches

Salads

Chicken

Beef

Pork

Fish and Seafood

Vegetarian

Wild Game

Side Dishes

Desserts and Breads

641.56   spiral   PBK
Eukel   57, 415

Eukel, Sandra

Sensibly Thin

Mar 12 '98	DATE DUE		
Nov 24 '98	Jan 3 '99	Feb 22 2011	
Oct 7 '98	Feb 26 01	MAR. 8 2011	
De 18 '98	JUN 2 0 2009		
Jan 14 '99	JUL 2 0 2009		
Fe 8 '99	NOV 1 0 2010		
Mar 1 '99	NUV 3 0 2010		
Mar 9 '99	DEC 14 10		
May 24 '99	DEC 28-10		
May 25 '99	JAN 11 - 11		
6/1/10	JAN 24 - 11		
Jun 30 '99	Feb 7 - 11		